THE JEW CALLED
JESUS

THE JEW CALLED
JESUS

ROBERT CROTTY

Photographs by Michael Coyne

E. J. DWYER
DAVID LOVELL

First published in 1993 by
E.J. Dwyer (Australia) Pty Ltd
3/32-72 Alice Street
Newtown NSW 2042
Australia
Ph: (02) 550 2355
Fax: (02) 519 3218

in association with
David Lovell Publishing
308 Victoria Street
Brunswick VIC 3056

National Library of Australia
Cataloguing-in-Publication data

Crotty, Robert B.
  The Jew called Jesus.

  ISBN 0 85574 157 0.

  1. Jesus Christ - Bibliography - Juvenile literature. 2. Jesus Christ -
Jewishness - Juvenile literature. 3. Jesus Christ - Historicity -
Juvenile literature. 4. Jesus Christ - Jewish interpretations - Juvenile
literature. I. Coyne, Michael. II. Title.

232.9

Cover design by Stanley Wong
Text design by Stanley Wong
Typeset in 11½/13 pt Korinna by Post Typesetters, Brisbane

Distributed in Canada by:

Meakin and Associates
Unit 17
81 Auriga Drive
NEPEAN, ONT K2E 7Y5
Ph: (613) 226 4381

Distributed in Ireland and the U.K. by:

Columba Book Service
93 The Rise
Mount Merrion
BLACKROCK CO. DUBLIN
Ph. (01) 283 2954

Distributed in the United States by:

Morehouse Publishing
871 Ethan Allen Highway
RIDGEFIELD CT 06877
Ph: (203) 431 3927

Printed in Singapore by Arico Printers Pte Ltd

Contents

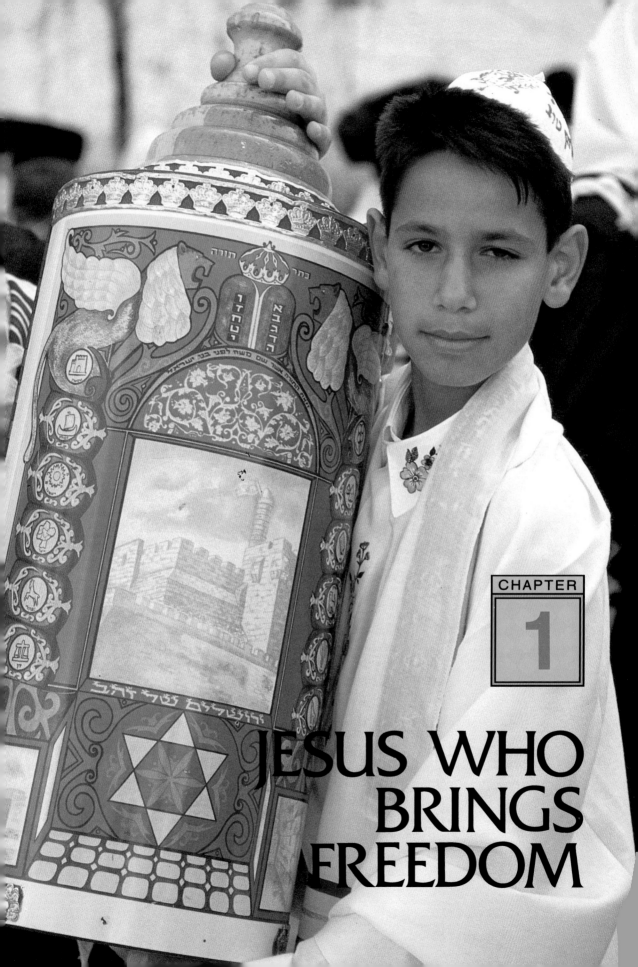

JESUS WHO BRINGS FREEDOM

This book has been written to give you some ideas about Jesus of Nazareth. Jesus was brought up in a small town in an area called Galilee. The town was Nazareth. It is still there today, although we are not exactly sure where Jesus' house or street were. The people of Galilee were looked upon by others of their time as rough and unsophisticated. People laughed at the accent they had when they spoke. They were Jews and that is important. Jesus, too, was a Jew. Our first task will be to find out a little more about the Jews and that is the purpose of the conversation that follows.

A conversation with Jeremy

Just a few days ago Jeremy celebrated his bar mitzvah. Jeremy is thirteen and is Jewish. We do not have the opportunity to learn about Judaism very often, so it seemed a good idea to ask him about this important ceremony in a Jew's life. Here is our conversation with Jeremy.

US: Jeremy, what does bar mitzvah mean?

JEREMY: Bar mitzvah is a very special ceremony which Jewish boys take part in when we are thirteen. The words are Hebrew and mean 'son of the commandment'. Now that I have had my bar mitzvah it means that I must keep all the traditions of Judaism. I am no longer a child; I am an adult now.

US: What does being Jewish mean?

JEREMY: I was born a Jew because my mother is Jewish. In fact, my mother and father are both Jewish and my grandparents are Jewish. We can trace our ancestors right back to the Jews of old, to Abraham, Isaac and Jacob. We all belong to a people who once made a covenant with God.

US: We don't understand that word 'covenant'.

JEREMY: A covenant is a treaty or an agreement. Sometimes people who are buying and selling land today still use it in the contracts they draw up. We Jews use it to describe a special agreement between ourselves and God. God agreed to be our God and we agreed to be his people. When Jewish boys are eight days old we have a special operation performed on us and the foreskin of our penis is removed. This is called circumcision. It means that we have been accepted into the covenant group, the people with whom God has a special agreement.

(Previous page) A young man holds the scroll of the Torah in a proud moment after his bar mitzvah.

US: Tell us something more about this bar mitzvah.

JEREMY: Well, last Saturday, which we call Shabbat or the Sabbath, which is the seventh day of the week, I went to the synagogue...

US: I'm afraid we don't really understand that word either.

JEREMY: A synagogue is something like a church. It's a special holy place put aside for the study of the Bible and for prayer. The word is actually a Greek one and means a 'meeting place', which describes what it is used for. I went to the synagogue in my best suit over which I wore a *tallit*.

US: You've caught us out again. What's a *tallit*?

JEREMY: A *tallit* is a prayer shawl. Jewish men wear it when they pray. I know some Jews who wear one under their shirts every day to show that they are always ready to pray. It has fringes on it to remind us to keep the commandments of God. I also had a little cap called a *kippa* on my head.

US: What happened at the synagogue?

JEREMY: The Rabbi, who is something like a minister or priest,

A group gathers to celebrate a bar mitzvah at the Western Wall in the Old City of Jerusalem.

welcomed us all. Then a Cantor, who is in charge of the singing, went to the cabinet which contains the scrolls of the Torah. We call the first five books of the Bible the Torah.

The Cantor took out a Torah scroll written by hand on parchment and he said: 'Blessed be He who in his Holiness gave the Torah to his people, Israel.' All the people in the synagogue then recited the great prayer of the Torah, called the Shema. It begins like this:

> Hear, O Israel, the Lord our God, the Lord is one.
> And you shall love the Lord your God with all your heart
> and with all your soul and with all your might.

Then I felt very nervous because I had to go up next to the Rabbi and read the Bible passage for the day in Hebrew.

US: Is Hebrew a difficult language?

JEREMY: Not so difficult. It has fewer letters in its alphabet than English. However, you do have to read from the right to the left instead of the way we read English. But it's the language of my people and really want to learn it.

I read part of the story from the Bible about Moses leading the Israelites from Egypt. The Rabbi said I did it very well and he then spoke to the people about the meaning of my bar mitzvah. Finally he gave everyone the special Jewish blessing which goes like this:

The young man celebrating his bar mitzvah reads one of the prayers.

May the Lord bless you and keep you
May the Lord make his face shine upon you
    and be gracious to you.
May the Lord lift up his face upon you
    and give you peace.

The scroll of the Torah is held up for all to see.

US: What happened after you left the synagogue?

JEREMY: After it was all over my father and mother gave a party for our family and friends. I had to give a speech and thank everyone for helping me to understand my Jewish faith. I also thanked them all for the presents they had brought me.

US: Will your sister, Sarah, have a bar mitzvah too?

JEREMY: Bar mitzvah used to be for boys only. When my mother was a girl there was nothing for girls. But things are changing. Next year, when my sister is thirteen, she will have a bat mitzvah. 'Bat' means 'daughter' and so bat mitzvah means 'daughter of the commandment'. The ceremony is the same as for boys. Not all Jewish groups have the bat mitzvah but more and more are doing so.

US: Thanks so much, Jeremy, for explaining everything to us.

WHAT ABOUT CHRISTIANS?

JEREMY: There are some things I don't understand about you Christian people, you know. For example, what happens when you Christians are baptised?

US: (In your own words give an answer to Jeremy. You might like to ask your parents about your own baptism.)

JEREMY: Circumcision means we become part of the Jewish people and its long, long history. Does baptism mean something the same to Christians?

US: (Try to answer Jeremy's new question)

JEREMY: What about your confirmation? What happens when someone is confirmed?

US: (What would you answer to this one?)

JEREMY: Does that mean that confirmation is much the same as a bar mitzvah or a bat mitzvah?

US: (Can you give him an answer?)

JEREMY: I must be going. When we part we Jews say Shalom. It means 'hello', 'goodbye' and also 'peace'.

US: Shalom, Jeremy

Talking with Jeremy may have given you some ideas about Judaism and about Jews. That's important for this book. Jesus was a Jew. He was born as a Jew. He died a Jew. He was circumcised. He studied the Torah. He was sometimes called Rabbi. We want to stress the fact, in this book, that Jesus was a Jew and that the Christian faith began within Judaism. Jews and Christians are very close.

We need to learn something more about Judaism before we can go more deeply into Jesus' story.

The Jewish Story

Jewish people look back to a great leader called Moses. When Egypt was still a powerful nation and before the time of the Greeks and the Romans, there had been a people living in a land called Canaan. They were the Children of Israel or the Israelites. They were a people who looked back to great ancestors called Abraham, Isaac and Jacob. (These were mentioned by Jeremy in his conversation earlier.) They were not important as far as the rest of world history goes. They were not able to mount an army to fight the Egyptians.

Because there was a great shortage of food in their land they had been forced to go down to Egypt. It was a mysterious land. Hundreds of years earlier the Egyptians had built the pyramids as tombs for their kings, the pharaohs. Great temples dotted the land. The pharaohs ruled not only the land of Egypt but other lands distant from them.

At first the Israelites were treated kindly. They were given their own area of land in which to live. They settled there for hundreds of years. However one particular pharaoh turned the Egyptians against them.

They came not to trust the Israelites. They were afraid that the Israelites might assist their enemies. They made them prisoners in the land of Egypt and forced them to become their slaves. They treated them cruelly. All Israelite male children had to be killed at birth. There did not seem to be any hope.

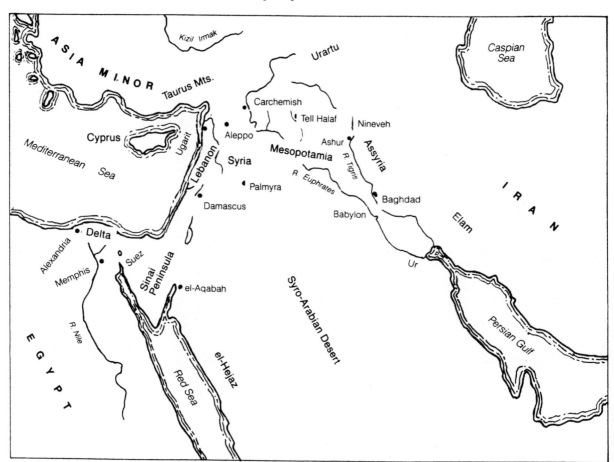

THE NEAR EAST
in Ancient Times

Would the people of Israel disappear from history for all time? It was just then that there appeared a great hero called Moses. He was an Israelite but he had been brought up by an Egyptian princess. He saw his own people being enslaved and he decided to do something for them. He believed in God who would save the people. He was certain that God would deliver them. He asked the pharaoh if he could lead them back to their own land in Canaan. Only after the pharaoh and the Egyptians had been terribly punished by God did they allow the Israelites to return to their own land. The return of the people of Israel is called the Exodus, which means an exit from Egypt. Moses led the people out. The Egyptians tried to follow but God again protected them.

At a sacred mountain in the desert, called Mount Sinai, a very important religious ceremony took place. Moses climbed to the top of the mountain. God, who could not be seen by humans, spoke to

Moses. Then Moses took the message of God back to the people who were waiting at the foot of the mountain. The message was that they were to be the special people of God and he was to be their God. They were to obey what God commanded them to do and God would protect them. This agreement was called the covenant. It was as if God and the Israelites had made a treaty or agreement between themselves. They were the people of the covenant.

Moses led the people through the dry and harsh desert. He died just as they reached the land called Canaan. The people entered the land of Canaan and fought against the tribes who lived there. When the war was won they settled down. They called themselves the people of God. In that land they were later to build a great Temple in the city of Jerusalem where God would be worshipped and honored.

JUDAISM

The religion of these Israelites came to be called Judaism. The district around Jerusalem was called Judea and that is where the word 'Judaism' comes from. Jews are people who follow the religion of Judaism. Jews believe that God protects them and protects all peoples. They believe that just as God took pity on the Israelites in Egypt and allowed Moses to set them free and lead them into their own land, so he will always look after his people while they are true to the covenant. He will raise up other leaders to lead them just as Moses did.

The Jewish people are certainly not without troubles today. Soldiers are a prominent sight around Jerusalem, here resting at a market by the Damascus Gate.

Hundreds of years after their time in Egypt the Israelites were again suffering. No longer was it the Egyptians who were oppressing them. It was other nations from the area in which they lived. Assyrians and Babylonians from Mesopotamia had come with great armies and laid siege to their cities. Many had been killed and many cities had been destroyed. Persians had allowed the Jews to rebuild the holy city of Jerusalem but they would not allow them to govern themselves. Then the Greeks had arrived. They tried to force the Israelites to give up the worship of God altogether. They killed young Jewish men and women because they would not worship Greek gods. Finally came the Romans. The Roman army took over their cities and they ruled their land.

● Try now to imagine your-self in the world of the Jews in this ancient period. Have a good look at this diagram of the world.

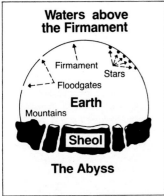

The Ancient Hebrew view of the World

Of course, people today do not believe that the world looks like this, but two or three thousand years ago most people saw the world in this way. Read Genesis chapter 1 in a Bible and see if you can understand it with the help of the diagram. Redraw this world and put in some of the statements from Genesis 1.

● In this world the Jews saw many enemies. Describe how you see the world using these words: Satan, devil, angel, Spirit. Write a colorful paragraph.

● Pretend that you are Jeremy, whom you met before, and who expects that the Messiah is still to come. Write a paragraph about Jews expecting the Messiah.

EVIL vs GOOD

The world for the Jewish people was at this time a terrible place. There was suffering, there was persecution. There was the death of loved ones. When they spoke about the world they described it as a good land but one that had come under the power of evil forces. Evil could almost be touched. Evil made Greeks and Romans oppress the Jews. They spoke about the forces of Good and the forces of Evil. These two forces were at battle in the world. God led the forces of Good. He was helped by his angels (his messengers). Angels carried out his commands and helped the people of Israel. Satan (a word which means Enemy) was the leader of the forces of Evil. He hated the people of Israel and he, with his followers, the demons, influenced Greeks and Romans to persecute the Jews.

The people of Israel looked to God. He seemed, though, to be far away. He was doing nothing for them. Sometimes they described him as a Spirit or Wind. Just as a great wind or storm would arise and stir up the land so they wanted God to change things for them. They spoke about him as a God-Spirit or Spirit of Holiness. Here is one prayer they addressed to him:

> O God, please open up the sky and come down to us.
> Even the mountains will then tremble because of you.
> It will be like when fire sets dry wood alight
>   or when fire boils water.
> At that time your enemies will realise who you are
> and other peoples will shake with fear because of you.

They were waiting for another Moses who would come and lead them. Moses had saved the Israelites in ancient times from their enemy—Egypt. The New Moses, whom they called the Messiah (which means 'Anointed One'), would once again, they were sure, free God's people. When we translate Messiah from Hebrew to Greek we get the word *Christos* or Christ. They were awaiting the Christ.

THE MESSIAH

Moses had led the people of Israel through the desert of Sinai. The people expected that the New Moses, the Messiah, would come out of the desert once again. He would save them just as Moses had saved their ancestors.

But how were they to know when the Messiah was to come? And how would they recognize the Messiah when he arrived? In their ancient writings, in the Torah, there were some clues. A prophet, a holy man very close to God, called Isaiah, had written about a strange Voice that had announced:

In the desert make a path for God.
In the wilderness make a straight road for our God.

The Jews concluded that there must be someone who would come before the Messiah and prepare the way. He would be a Forerunner. The Forerunner would prepare the people and ensure that there was a group ready to welcome the Messiah. If they could recognise the Forerunner they would know that the Messiah was soon to come.

The Christian Story

Let us now look at how Christians fit in. We are going to read from the Christian story. This is called the New Testament.

In the New Testament there are twenty-seven books. Some are letters and four are collections of stories called gospels. The gospels have come down to us written in the Greek language, but you will read them in English, in a translation specially written for you.

You will need to take note of what has been said about Judaism above if you are to understand what the gospels have to say. You must remember that they were written for people who sometimes were Jews or at least lived in a world where Jews were well known. Most importantly, they were written about the Jew named Jesus.

We will look first at one of the gospels, the one written by Mark.

The gospel of Mark begins in this way:

THIS IS AN ACCOUNT
OF THE GOOD NEWS
CONCERNING JESUS THE MESSIAH.

That is the title. 'Good News' was a special word. When one of the Greek kings in those days wanted to make an important announcement he would send off a messenger who had learned the message by heart. It might be a message announcing that the king's son would marry, that the king had won a great victory in war, that the taxes would soon go up. The message was called the Good News. The Christians likened God to a king. He had a message for humans. It was Good News. The message was that Jesus was the Messiah or the Christ. Everything would be changed. The world was about to undergo a revolution.

THE FORERUNNER

A man called John the Baptizer came into the desert. He told about a baptism for those people who had changed their whole way of living. This baptism showed that sins were now forgiven. All the people from the Judean area and from the city of Jerusalem came out to him. They were baptized by him in the river Jordan. But first they had to acknowledge that they had been sinful. John wore clothes made of camel hair, with a leather belt around his waist. He ate locusts and wild honey. He preached this message:

'Someone even more important than me is going to arrive later than me. I am not worthy to untie this person's sandals. I have baptized you with water. He is going to baptize you with the Spirit of Holiness'.

Christians still come from all over the world so they can be baptized in the River Jordan.

You can tell that the writer of the gospel thinks that John the Baptizer was the Forerunner, that he was the one spoken of by Isaiah. Many Jews did not agree. Jeremy would not agree today.

Mark shows us all the evidence. John is in the desert. He is dressed like one of the ancient prophets in camel hair clothes. He eats the food of the desert region. He is baptizing. Baptism for John was a special ceremony which singled out the people who would be ready to welcome the Messiah. John must be the Forerunner.

THE BAPTISM OF JESUS

Jesus, from Nazareth in Galilee, arrived about this time. He too was baptized by John in the Jordan. But just as he came up out of the water, he saw the sky above him open and the Spirit of God come down upon him in the form of a dove. A Voice was heard coming from the sky: 'You are my Beloved Son. I am delighted with you.'

Mark reveals the secret message of the Good News. Jesus is the Messiah. That is why we often refer to him as Jesus Christ. It simply means Jesus Messiah. Remember how the Jews were praying for God to do something, to open the sky and act. Mark tells his readers that God has done just that. He has acted in a new way. He has sent Jesus into the world.

THE TESTING OF JESUS

Straightaway the Spirit sent Jesus into the desert. He was in that desert for a very long time. Satan struggled with him. He lived among wild animals. Angels looked after his needs.

Remember what the Jews believed about the battle between Good and Evil. Jesus is to do battle with Satan. The leader of the forces of Good is to fight the leader of the forces of Evil. This is why Jesus came into the world. You can see why you need to understand Mark's use of the words 'Spirit of Holiness', 'Messiah', 'Satan', 'angels' and even 'desert'. Otherwise none of this may make good sense.

JESUS' ANNOUNCEMENT

After John had been arrested Jesus came into Galilee. He announced the Good News of God. He said, 'The time has finally arrived! God's Kingdom is here! Change your life and accept the Good News.'

John's role as Forerunner is over. He is arrested by the Jewish king called Herod, who was not a practising Jew and who had been put in place by the Romans, and later put to death. Jesus begins to travel around the whole country announcing the Good News. It is exciting times.

THE CALL OF THE FIRST DISCIPLES

As he walked along the Sea of Galilee he saw Simon and his brother Andrew. They were throwing a net into the sea. They fished for their living. Jesus said to them, 'Follow me and I'll make you fish for people!' They left their nets at once and they followed him.
    When he had walked just a little further he saw James, Zebedee's son, and his brother John. They were mending nets in their boat. He called out to them. They left Zebedee, their father, in the boat with some servants and they too went off with Jesus.

The work of Jesus had now begun in earnest. Jesus must have been a very attractive preacher. He called people. They were enthralled by him. They might not yet realize what following him would involve but still they left everything and followed him. Jesus and his followers together would spread the Good News.

Jesus' message today

We have now seen something about the Jewish people and the religion of Judaism to which Jesus belonged. Remember though that Judaism isn't just a religion from ancient times. There are Jews *today*. We can learn a great deal from them about Jesus and about Christianity.

We want to think about what we have learned about Jesus. He was a person who brought the Good News. It meant a great deal to the people of his day. What does it mean today?

Jesus came to his people, the Jews, just at a time when they were suffering as they had never suffered before. In the gospel of Luke we read that Jesus once went into a synagogue on a Sabbath day and did the reading, just as young Jeremy did on his bar mitzvah. Jesus selected the reading. It was from the prophecy of Isaiah and it read:

The Spirit of the Lord has come down upon me.
He has anointed me.
He has sent me to announce Good News
     to the oppressed peoples,
to proclaim that prisoners will be released,
     that blind people will be given back their sight,
     that those who have been crushed down will be freed.

Now let us see some cases where Jesus has affected people's lives.

MATTHEW THE TAX COLLECTOR

Matthew was a tax collector who lived at the same time as Jesus.
Nowadays people who work for a tax office are quite respectable. They
have an important job to perform for the government and they usually
do it very well. However, in the days of Jesus things were very different.

     You recall that the Romans were in control of the land of Israel.
They needed taxes to keep their Empire going. A good part of the tax

went back to Rome and it helped to finance the running of the great Roman Empire. Jews who wanted to be tax collectors had to work on behalf of the Romans, to demand tax from their own people. Worse still, once the amount of money required by the Romans was gathered the tax collectors were free to collect any more for themselves. You can understand how much they were hated by other people! Other Jews were not even permitted to eat with the tax collectors.

This was the situation Matthew found himself in. He was one of the hated tax collectors. One day, Jesus saw Matthew in his tax office. Poor Matthew. He needed to make a living and yet he was rejected by his Jewish friends; he was forbidden to go to the synagogue. Jesus went up to him and very quietly said, 'Follow me.' Matthew got up and left everything behind him and followed Jesus.

Matthew found a new freedom by following Jesus. No doubt he had heard of Jesus. Jesus had been going around preaching, healing and bringing peace into the lives of many people. When Matthew heard Jesus' words he realized that this was the opportunity he had been waiting for. For Matthew, Jesus brought freedom.

ARCHBISHOP DESMOND TUTU

Archbishop Desmond Tutu is an Anglican archbishop in South Africa. He is black. In fact most of the people in South Africa are black, yet the government is controlled by whites. White people earn more money, get better jobs, are educated better, have better hospitals. Black people often live in poverty. Once they were even forbidden to sit on the same seats as white people, use the same beaches, eat in the same restaurants. This separation of whites and blacks is called *apartheid*. Apartheid meant persecution of the blacks. The government in South Africa used to say that this was for the greater good of blacks and whites. But it meant suffering and hardship for the blacks.

Archbishop Tutu does not believe that the world should be divided into blacks and whites. He does not believe that black people should be imprisoned in their own country. He will not accept apartheid. He believes that the coming of Jesus means freedom for all people—whether they are Jews or not Jews, males or females, black or white.

He does not believe in violence but he does believe that he should stand up in his cathedral in South Africa and announce that Jesus would not today accept apartheid. He leads marches to demand that black people be given freedom, a freedom equal to the whites. For him Jesus means freedom.

South Africa is changing. Black people are discovering freedom. The white government is beginning to change its attitude. Part of the reason for the change is that Archbishop Tutu has fearlessly announced the Good News that Jesus brought.

- *Now it is time for an activity. Sit quietly for a few minutes and think about people you know today. Are they free? Try to put down on paper the ways in which they are not free. Now form small groups and share what you have written. Listen carefully to each person in your small group.*

- *Now come together as a class. You have a new question. If Jesus were to speak today what would he say about this lack of freedom? Let different people have a say.*

- *Can anything be done about the situation? In pairs design a poster that shows what you think can be done. You could, for example, show a black person and a white person working or playing together. You could show someone consoling an unhappy child or feeding a hungry person, helping a homeless person to build a new home. There are so many ways in which freedom can be brought into our world.*

JESUS WHO WAS BORN IN BETHLEHEM

e have learned something about the background of Jesus, but where did Jesus come from? We would certainly like to know everything about his beginnings. However he lived a long time ago. We must be satisfied that there will be a lot about his early days that is unknown. What stories we do know have come down over a long period of time.

We cannot be sure that the gospel stories give us the exact details about the life of Jesus. Sometimes the gospels contradict each other. The gospels are collections of memories that have been cleverly put together to give a good overall impression of who Jesus was and what he accomplished. They do not pretend to be a strict history of events. We are going to read them as stories, stories which are mostly a true record of events, but whose main purpose is to present God's message of Good News in Jesus.

Those stories would have meant a great deal to the early Christians. No doubt you have stories about the early days of those you love, your family.

We will begin some reflection on the birth of Jesus by listening to the ways in which people from many parts of the world celebrate the birth of Jesus today and have celebrated his birth for a long time.

Family Focus

● *Draw each of your family as babies (perhaps you are lucky enough to have baby photos you can use). Under each one put that person's date and place of birth and some story or memory about their early days. Find out if there are any memories about you when you were a baby that your family still hand on.*

Christmas around the world

THE FIRST PEOPLE TO CELEBRATE CHRISTMAS

When we go back to the early days of the Christian era we find that in ancient Rome 25 December was the Birthday of the Unconquered Sun. The Romans worshipped the Unconquered Sun God. It was the sun that brought them warmth, light and good crops. Towards the end of December they knew that the winter solstice occurred. The solstice marks the time of the year when the days start to become longer. People thought that was the time the sun renewed itself and came closer to the land. From then on the weather became warmer. The Romans celebrated the sun's return. The feasting began on 17 December with processions in which both men and women adorned themselves with evergreen wreaths around their heads and carried candles.

We think that the early Christians may have taken advantage of these celebrations to honor Jesus. At first they were forced to honor him in private because they were sometimes persecuted by the Romans and they had to keep out of public view. However, on 25 December *everyone* in Rome rejoiced. Who could have told the difference if Christians were rejoicing too?

(Previous page) A shepherd leads his flock out to pasture. It was the shepherds who received the announcement of Jesus' birth on Christmas night.

Then, under the Emperor Constantine the Great, Christianity was allowed to be practised. Under one of his successors, the Emperor Theodosius, it became the only religion to be followed throughout the whole Empire. The 25th of December became the official birthday of Jesus and the Sun God was forgotten.

Yet, some of the old customs continued. Evergreen wreaths and decorations had been used for the feast of the Sun. Now they were used to honor Jesus. Holly with its red berries was one of the few evergreens to have a decorative look in the cold winter countryside and so holly became a part of Christmas. In the Old English language, the celebration became known as *Christes Masse*, the Mass of Christ, referring to the Mass or the Eucharist that celebrated the birth of Jesus on that day. So Christmas came to be.

AN ENGLISH CHRISTMAS

St Augustine came to England with forty monks in the year 596 CE to introduce Christianity. From this time the celebration of Christmas on 25 December took hold of the English countryside. The day has always been one of celebration, of family reunions and joy. Christmas trees are erected in churches and homes.

Since the Second World War a large Christmas tree stands in the very centre of London, in Trafalgar Square, a gift sent each year by the people of Norway to thank the people of Britain for what they did for them during that war. On Christmas Eve groups of singers go from house to house singing Christmas carols. Children send letters to Father Christmas by throwing them in the fireplace (fires are always needed during an English winter) and watching them go up the chimney. Traditionally, an English Christmas dinner includes turkey or perhaps goose, vegetables, mince pies and plum pudding.

Countries that were settled by people from Britain, such as the United States, New Zealand and Australia, celebrate Christmas in similar ways.

LET'S GO TO ITALY FOR CHRISTMAS

The Christmas season in Italy begins eight days before 25 December. Children are taught to recite Christmas poems and sing hymns. Shepherds come to the cities from the countryside and play Christmas songs on reed pipes. A very noticeable feature is the crib. Cribs are models of the stable where Jesus was born. Jesus is in his child's bed or crib which had been the feeding stall for the animals. Other figures are Mary and Joseph, sheep, oxen, shepherds and the Wise Men. Cribs are to be found in homes and especially in churches. Some of them are elaborate with moving parts: the Wise Men bow, fountains play, sheep baa, Joseph looks about.

Christmas Day is a day when most Italians go to church to attend Mass. Gifts are not given on this day. Italian children receive gifts on 6 January, which is called the feast of the Epiphany. Instead of a Father Christmas Italians have an ugly looking witch called La Befana who delivers presents. Legend says that she was told by the shepherds of the wonderful happenings in Bethlehem. The Star of Bethlehem was even pointed out to her. She delayed setting out and missed seeing Jesus. Since then she has searched the world for him. She leaves presents at each home in the hope that Jesus might be there.

SOMETHING GOOD TO EAT AT CHRISTMAS

Italians have special recipes for Christmas. Here's one for biscuits called *Amaretti*:

  2 egg whites
  ¼ teaspoon salt
  1 cup sugar
  1 cup chopped blanched almonds
  ¾ teaspoon almond extract

Add the salt to the egg whites and then beat until frothy. Add the sugar, beating until the mixture is stiff. Add the almonds and the almond extract and fold them in gently. Drop the almond mixture on to a buttered and floured baking tray. Shape into small mounds. Let them stand for two hours. Bake at 190°C for twelve minutes until they are a nice brown color.

HOW WOULD A GREEK CHRISTIAN CELEBRATE CHRISTMAS?

Christmas Day in Greece is a day of feasting and celebration but not a day for giving gifts. Gifts come at New Year and St Basil is said to bring them. On Christmas Eve boys move from house to house singing carols. They are rewarded with packets of sweets and nuts. It is traditional to have certain foods: there is *Christopsomo*, a bread twisted into the form of animals and Christmas biscuits. Some food is left outside for the *kalikantzari*, the evil goblins who are said to wander about.

• *Describe how Christmas is celebrated in your home. Illustrate your description with a drawing of the occasion. Use plenty of color. In small groups share your descriptions.*

JUST WHO WAS SANTA CLAUS?

Saint Nicholas was an archbishop who lived in Asia Minor (which today is called Turkey) between 271 and 342 CE. He loved children and became a favourite saint in Greece and Russia. Many stories are told

about Saint Nicholas but the best known is that he heard that the three daughters of a poor man were to be sold as slaves because their father did not have any money. They could not get married without money for their husbands. Nicholas tossed three bags of gold through their window. One bag landed in a stocking that was hanging by the chimney to dry. Saint Nicholas was the first Father Christmas and the Father Christmas costume of today is a copy of the bishop's white robe, scarlet cape and red mitre.

The first Christmas

You can see that celebrating Christmas is important to many people in many different ways. What can we find out about the first Christmas, the birth of Jesus in Bethlehem?

THE BIRTHPLACE OF JESUS

Jesus, the story tells us, was born in Bethlehem. Today Bethlehem is a small town just south of Jerusalem. Most of the people who live there are Arabs. Some of the Arabs are Christian and others are Muslim. They all feel very proud to live in the town where Jesus was born. In the fourth century the Roman emperor Constantine built a large church or basilica over a cave where Jesus was said to have been born. The gospels do not mention a cave and Matthew, as we will see, says that Jesus was born in a house in Bethlehem. However some early Christian writers do mention a cave. Even today many houses in Bethlehem are built in front of a cave which is used to store goods and farm animals.

The very low door leading into the Church of the Nativity in Bethlehem.

Another Roman emperor called Justinian in the sixth century ordered his ruler in Bethlehem to pull down the basilica that Constantine had built and to build another that would be outstanding in size and beauty.

Later the Crusaders, Christian soldiers who came to fight the Arabs, found this basilica in a poor state of repair and they rebuilt it in the eleventh and twelfth centuries. It now has a very low doorway, so small that those entering must stoop down to get into the basilica. Why? Some say it was to make everyone bow low before entering the birthplace of Jesus. Some say it was to ensure that the Crusaders got off their horses before entering, others say it was to stop people driving carts into the basilica and stealing its valuables. It is called the Door of Humility.

Inside the basilica there are four rows of columns built of reddish limestone. Descending some steps you come to a cave under the basilica with its walls plastered. It is dark and smoky because there are lots of candles. A large star on the floor indicates where tradition says Jesus was born. Inscribed on the floor are the words: *Hic de Virgine Maria Jesus Christus Natus Est.* ('At this place Jesus Christ was born of the Virgin Mary.')

Today three groups of Christians look after the basilica in Bethlehem. There are Greek Orthodox, Catholics and Armenians. They all hold services regularly in the basilica.

Just outside of Bethlehem there is Rachel's Tomb. You will hear of Rachel in the gospel story which remembers her from the Hebrew Scriptures of the Jewish people. She was the favourite wife of the great father of the people of Israel, Jacob. He had three other wives as was allowed in those days. After her death Jacob set up a memorial pillar on her grave and that pillar is still supposed to be there today.

Now it is time to hear from Matthew's gospel what took place in Bethlehem. This is just one of the stories that the early Christians told about the birth of Jesus. Luke has another story which is somewhat different. We could read either one but on this occasion we will read Matthew's story.

THE BIRTH OF JESUS

This is the story about the birth of Jesus the Messiah. His mother Mary was married to a man called Joseph. Before they had moved into their house together she discovered that she was going to have a baby. Her pregnancy had been brought about by the Spirit of Holiness.

Her husband Joseph kept the Jewish Law very strictly. He did not want her to be put to shame and so he decided to divorce her without any further fuss. He had quite made up his mind to do this when God's Angel appeared to him in a dream. The Angel said: 'Joseph, son of David, don't be afraid about taking your wife Mary into your home. She has become pregnant by the Spirit of Holiness. Her child will be a boy and you are to call him Jesus, because he is going to save his people from their sinfulness.'

(Over page) A donkey surveys the town of Bethlehem.

Now all of this took place according to what God had told his people through the prophet:

> The Virgin will become pregnant
> and will have a son.
> He will be called Emmanuel.

This name means 'God is with us'.

When Joseph woke up he carried out the Angel of God's instructions and took Mary to his home although he did not have sexual intercourse with her before she gave birth to a baby boy. He was called Jesus.

The Church of the Nativity.

The first part of the story tells us about Jesus' birth. When we look at the birth stories of great people from other cultures we find that there is something similar. The great pharaohs of Egypt were said to have had one of the gods for their father. Great heroes of Israel were sometimes born to women who seemed to be far too old to have a child. Isaac's mother Sarah was afraid that people would laugh at her because she was as old as a grandmother but had a little baby. Birth stories often tell of wondrous births that could not have been expected.

This story tells of the marriage of Jesus' mother. In Israel two thousand years ago there were two steps to a marriage. Firstly the man and the woman (who usually was a girl about twelve or thirteen) came before witnesses and solemnly agreed that they would marry. Then the woman, although married at this point, went back to her parents' home. About one year later the husband would arrange for the wife to come to his home. This was the second step. In this case Mary had been married to Joseph but had not yet gone to his home. Divorce was allowed by the Law of Judaism. Because Mary was pregnant, and Joseph knew he was not the father of the child, he thought it necessary to divorce her.

The Christian birth story has four major characters (and some minor ones) besides Mary and Joseph. There is the 'Spirit of Holiness', who is God. There is the 'Angel of God' who is a messenger sent by God. When the Jewish people wanted to say that God talked to them they sometimes said that God sent his messenger or angel. Then there is the Prophet. Prophets were people who spoke on behalf of God. They sometimes sternly corrected the people and sometimes they consoled them. Matthew makes use of several prophets in his story. One prophet, Isaiah, had told his people of a coming child who would give the people cause for joy. Later on, some Jews thought that Isaiah must have been speaking of the Messiah and they understood him to have said that the Messiah would be born of a virgin, that is a woman who has never had sexual relations with a man.

Matthew often added sayings of one of the prophets into his stories. He wanted to show that Jesus' life followed on from the life of the people of Israel. So he 'stitched' sayings from the prophets into the life story of Jesus.

The fourth character is, of course, Jesus, whose name in Hebrew was Joshua and means 'Savior'. It was he who was going to save and deliver his people.

THE WISE MEN FROM THE EAST

Jesus was born in Bethlehem in the land of Judea. His birth took place when Herod was king. Wise men from the East arrived in Jerusalem. They enquired: 'Where is the newborn king of the Jews? We saw his star rising and we came to worship him.' When King Herod heard this he was quite taken back. So, too, was the whole of Jerusalem. Herod gathered together all the chief priests and the scholars before him and asked them where the Messiah was going to be born. They informed him:

'In Bethlehem of Judea, because that is what the prophet wrote:

And you, Bethlehem, in the land of Judah,
You are the most powerful leader of Judah
Because a leader will come from you
Who will be the Shepherd of my people, Israel.'

Herod summoned the Wise Men to meet him in private. He enquired as to just when the star had appeared. Then he sent them off to Bethlehem. 'Go and find out everything you can about this child,' he said. 'When you have found him, come back and let me know so I too may go there and worship him myself.'

After listening to what the king had to say they set out on their journey. The star which they had seen rising still went ahead of them. Then, it came to a halt over the place where the child was lying. Seeing this star filled them with the greatest joy. They went into the house and saw the child and his mother, Mary. They bowed low, right down to the ground and then they paid him homage. They opened up their treasure boxes and they gave him gifts of gold, frankincense and myrrh.

They were warned in a dream not to go back again to Herod for he planned to find where he was and kill him. So they went home by a different road.

The story now introduces some new characters. These are the Wise Men. In the East, in what came to be called Mesopotamia, there were pagan priests. They were not Jews, although the Jews knew about them. They were said to have the power to interpret all sorts of signs, especially signs in the sky. There was another ancient belief that great people were welcomed into the world with a star at their birth. These priests had seen such a star and had followed it.

The other new character is an evil one. He was Herod the Great. Herod had been made the King of the Jews by the Romans who were in control of Palestine just then. He managed to keep the land safe and secure but at the same time he was very cruel. He murdered his wife and some of his own children. He started to rebuild the sacred Temple of Jerusalem, making it a huge and beautiful place. He died in 4 BCE.

THE FAMILY FLEES TO EGYPT AND RETURNS

Once the Wise Men had departed, the Angel of God again appeared in a dream to Joseph. He said: 'Get up and take the child and his mother and escape into Egypt. Stay there for as long as I tell you. Herod is going to search for this child to kill him.' Joseph got out of bed and got the child and his mother ready. By night they fled into Egypt. They remained there until Herod died. All of these events fulfilled what God had said through the prophet:

'I called my son out of Egypt.'

When Herod realised that the Wise Men had tricked him, he was absolutely furious. He ordered all boys aged two or younger living in Bethlehem and the nearby areas to be killed. He had worked out the time by his careful questioning of the Wise Men. This was the fulfilment of the saying of Jeremiah the prophet:

A star in the floor of the cave under the Church of the Nativity. It marks the spot where tradition says Jesus was born.

'A voice was heard in Ramah,
Wailing and bitterly moaning.
Rachel was weeping for her children
And she would not be comforted
Because they were gone.'

When Herod had died the Angel of God appeared in a dream to Joseph who was still down in Egypt. He said: 'Get up and take the child and his mother back to the land of Israel. All the people who wanted to kill the child are now dead.' Joseph got up and took the child and his mother back to the land of Israel.

However, when Joseph learned that Archelaus was now the king of Judea in place of his father, Herod, he was afraid to go there. After receiving a warning in a dream he set out for the Galilee district. Up there he settled in a town called Nazareth. This fulfilled the saying of the prophets:

'He shall be called a Nazorean.'

We will soon see that *nazorean* can mean several things. The people who first read Matthew's gospel would not have been sure at first what exactly was meant. We will continue the story and come back to the name.

The family fled to Egypt. Egypt was always looked upon as a good place for refugees, people fleeing from cruel rulers. Since 30 BCE it had been under the control of Rome, but there were many places where the refugees could go. From Chapter 1 we know that Egypt was the place where the people of Israel in ancient times took refuge and there they were forced into slavery by the pharaoh. Now it is the King of the Jews, Herod, who is the oppressor. Look again at the map on p.8 to see how far the family had to journey.

The prophet Jeremiah had told of Rachel, the mother of the tribe of Benjamin, weeping over the people who had descended from her son. They had been deported to a foreign country by the Assyrians in the eighth century. She was said to have been buried near Bethlehem and now Matthew tells of her weeping over the children killed by Herod.

At Herod's death the kingdom was divided up among his three sons. One of these was Archelaus. He too was a tyrant who killed many

of his own people. Some Jews even went to Rome and asked that he be removed as ruler. Matthew tells us that Joseph decided to go to Galilee in the north because of his fear of this Archelaus. This is how Jesus, although he was born in Bethlehem, was brought up in Nazareth which is in Galilee.

Finally Matthew bestows a new title on Jesus—he is a *Nazorean*. This was a very clever thing to say because it would have meant different things to the Jews of that time. Jesus was a Nazarene, which means that he was brought up in Nazareth, and Matthew has explained how he came to live in Nazareth although being born, as prophesied, in Bethlehem. 'Nazarene' and 'Nazorean' are close in sound.

Isaiah had also said that the Messiah would be a 'branch' coming from the 'Root of Jesse'. Jesse was the father of King David, one of the great ancestors of the Jews. You need to think of a tree from which a new branch has grown. The tree is Israel and Matthew is claiming that the new branch is Jesus. In Hebrew the word for 'branch' is *nezer* and that too sounds something like 'Nazorean'. Also some of the great people of Israel, for example Samson and Samuel, were known as a *nazir* or Holy Person. This also sounded something like Nazorean.

So, saying that Jesus was a Nazorean could be taken to mean all of the following: Jesus came from Nazareth, he was the new Branch expected by Israel and he was a Holy Person.

Reading and understanding that story should have really tested your minds. Now here is something practical for you to do!

(Over page) Looking across the fields to the town of Nazareth.

A Paraliturgy for the Birth of Jesus

Here is a paraliturgy for you. A paraliturgy is a form of prayer celebration. It celebrates the birth of Jesus but you do not have to wait for Christmas to use it. There are things to say, things to do, art work, colour, a little drama, sound, joy, peace.

The things to be said are provided for you. You will have to provide the rest for yourself. You will need first of all to go back over the text of the gospel of Matthew so that you can understand the speeches. So read what is written above very carefully. The rest is up to your imagination. You will need to do some art work—on the blackboard, a collage, posters perhaps. The color and the sound must be yours. Do you have any musical instruments? Most importantly, the joy and the peace are yours. You create them yourself. Try hard to make this *your* paraliturgy.

CHORUS
You, Bethlehem, in the land of Judah
You are the great leader of all Judah.
A leader will come from you
And he will be the Shepherd of Israel.

NARRATOR 1
Joseph was the son of Jacob, father of Israel.
He was the favourite of his father.
He could tell the meaning of dreams.
He was forced to go down to Egypt
Because his brothers were so jealous.
He lived there until those brothers came,
Forced by hunger to join him.

NARRATOR 2
Another Joseph was the husband of Mary.
His wife gave birth to a son,
Conceived by God's Spirit.
He too learned many things in dreams.
He was forced to go down to Egypt,
Taking his wife and the child.

CHORUS
A Virgin will conceive a child
And will have a son.
The son will be called Jesus.
He will free his people Israel.

NARRATOR 3

After many years there came an evil pharaoh
To the throne of Egypt.
He hated the people of Israel,
Ordering all their boys to be killed.
But one child was saved—the boy Moses.

NARRATOR 4

Herod was the evil king of the Jews.
Despised by the people of Israel.
He ordered all boys to be killed
In and around the town of Bethlehem.
But one child was saved—the boy Jesus.

CHORUS

A lonely voice is weeping.
It is Rachel weeping for her children.
Rachel cannot be comforted
Because her sons have gone.

NARRATOR 5

The child Moses was saved for a reason.
He was to lead his people Israel.
He led them on a great march
From Egypt to a new life and land.

NARRATOR 6

The child Jesus was saved for a reason.
He is the savior of his people.
He leads them on a great journey
And that journey continues still.

CHORUS

I called my son from Egypt.
I called my son to be the Branch
Of the Tree of Israel.
He is the Holy One of God.
He is Jesus from Nazareth.

CHAPTER 3

JESUS THE MESSIAH

n the last chapter we read of the birth of Jesus. The gospels give us no information about Jesus from the time he was a boy until he becomes a man. He grew up in Nazareth in Galilee and he was probably a carpenter like Joseph. When we next meet him he is no longer a carpenter but a preacher. He goes about doing good things. He preaches, he cures people who are ill, he casts out demons.

Today's preachers and healers

It is a little difficult for us to imagine what sort of a person Jesus was. Can we compare him to anyone we know today? We will have to do some thinking about that. If he was a preacher and a healer he may have been something like people who today preach and heal. So let us take a look at today's preachers and healers.

First of all we want to know what today's preachers and healers actually do. We have been fortunate enough to get two of them, one a Jew and the other a Christian, to tell us something about their work. They've kindly written a diary about a day in their lives. So, sit back and enjoy their description of what happens in their day.

DAILY DIARY OF A JEWISH RABBI

I'd like to introduce myself. I'm Rabbi David Cohen. I'm called 'Rabbi' by Jewish people as a mark of respect. It means 'My Teacher'. When I was a young man, I had to study very hard for a number of years in order to become a rabbi. Now I will describe what sort of things I do during my day.

Morning dawns. I begin each day with prayer. After I get up I put on my *tefillin*. These are two black leather boxes attached to black leather straps. Inside the small boxes (about the size of matchboxes) there are scraps of parchment with special readings from the Bible written on them. I wrap one strap around my head with the box on my forehead and another strap around my left arm and hand. Then I am ready to pray to my God, the God who long ago brought my people out of Egypt and gave us the Torah. One very special prayer begins like this:

> Hear, O Israel, the Lord is my God, the Lord is one. I praise my God, I pray for all my needs and the needs of my people Israel.

(Previous pages) Fishermen still find good catches in the Sea of Galilee.

Then I am ready to start the day.

After breakfast I go to the synagogue where I have an office. The synagogue is a Jewish house of prayer, something like a Christian church. Jews come there to pray, particularly on what we call Shabbat or Saturday. They also come there to study the Bible and other writings that have come down to us.

It is midmorning. On most weekdays, I have appointments. Some of the people in my congregation come to ask for advice or to talk about problems they may have with the Jewish observance. I have to make arrangements to talk with people who want to find out more about Judaism. I sometimes give talks to Christian groups and escort groups of school children and adults through the synagogue. Often people misunderstand Jews and Judaism.

I have to prepare Jewish children for their bar mitzvah and bat mitzvah. I also have to prepare for funerals when one of the people in my congregation has died. Every Jewish funeral requires a eulogy, a very personal talk about the life and achievements of the dead person. I also need some time to do my own study. We value the study of the Torah, of other Jewish writings and the Jewish religion very highly.

There are some very happy days when I perform the marriage service for young Jewish couples. The marriages usually take place in the synagogue. I stand opposite the groom who is under a small canopy, called a *chuppah*. The *chuppah* represents the groom's new home and when his bride comes into the synagogue she too stands under it. A special singer sings a greeting to them both, asking God's blessing. Then a cup of wine is poured and they both drink from it. The groom gives his bride a plain gold ring and he says, 'Behold you are made holy for me with this ring according to the law of Moses and Israel.' He then reads aloud his marriage vows. Together they share a second cup of wine and the groom stamps on and breaks a glass. The smashing of the glass is a sign that we Jews still mourn the loss of the city of Jerusalem and its Temple. The Romans destroyed it in the year 70 CE. All the people at the wedding call out 'Mazal tov' or 'Good luck'.

On Shabbat (which you remember is our name for our holy day, Saturday) there are two principal services in the synagogue. Shabbat really begins when the sun goes down on Friday night and lasts until the sun again sets on the Saturday night. The first service is on the Friday night and consists of readings from the Torah and special prayers. We welcome the arrival of our holy day.

Then on Saturday morning there is another service. At both services scrolls with books of the Bible written by hand are carefully and lovingly brought to a desk in the middle of the synagogue and then I or a special person called a cantor read from them. If there is a boy or girl who has just made bar mitzvah or bat mitzvah present then they will do the readings.

By now it is afternoon. After lunch I sometimes visit the sick from my congregation. I also run classes in the study of the Torah. One afternoon a week children from various schools come to the synagogue in order to learn the sacred language of Hebrew, the language in which the Bible was first written. This is what Hebrew looks like:

GENESIS. בראשית

א יִבְּרֵאשִׁית בָּרָא אֱלֹהִים אֵת הַשָּׁמַיִם וְאֵת הָאָרֶץ: יִוְהָאָרֶץ
הָיְתָה תֹהוּ וָבֹהוּ וְחֹשֶׁךְ עַל־פְּנֵי תְהוֹם וְרוּחַ אֱלֹהִים מְרַחֶפֶת עַל־פְּנֵי
הַמָּיִם: יוַיֹּאמֶר אֱלֹהִים יְהִי אוֹר וַיְהִי־אוֹר: יוַיַּרְא אֱלֹהִים אֶת־הָאוֹר
כִּי־טוֹב וַיַּבְדֵּל אֱלֹהִים בֵּין הָאוֹר וּבֵין הַחֹשֶׁךְ: יוַיִּקְרָא אֱלֹהִים לָאוֹר
יוֹם וְלַחֹשֶׁךְ קָרָא לָיְלָה וַיְהִי־עֶרֶב וַיְהִי־בֹקֶר יוֹם אֶחָד: פ

יוַיֹּאמֶר אֱלֹהִים יְהִי רָקִיעַ בְּתוֹךְ הַמָּיִם וִיהִי מַבְדִּיל בֵּין מַיִם לָמָיִם:
יוַיַּעַשׂ אֱלֹהִים אֶת־הָרָקִיעַ וַיַּבְדֵּל בֵּין הַמַּיִם אֲשֶׁר מִתַּחַת לָרָקִיעַ
וּבֵין הַמַּיִם אֲשֶׁר מֵעַל לָרָקִיעַ וַיְהִי־כֵן: יוַיִּקְרָא אֱלֹהִים לָרָקִיעַ שָׁמָיִם
וַיְהִי־עֶרֶב וַיְהִי־בֹקֶר יוֹם שֵׁנִי: פ   יוַיֹּאמֶר אֱלֹהִים יִקָּווּ הַמַּיִם

Night has come. After a long day I return to my family for dinner. We all say a blessing before we eat. We have some strict rules about what we can eat. We never eat pork, for example, because that is forbidden in the Torah. After dinner there are often meetings to attend. Every synagogue has a board of management to run its affairs. The board is elected by the members of my congregation and meets regularly.

My day, then is taken up with a good deal of work. I try to be a good person myself, a good Jew, and to help others.

The Western Wall, the only remaining part of the Second Temple. It is a most sacred place of pilgrimage and prayer for Jews the world over.

DAILY DIARY OF A CHRISTIAN MINISTER

I am a Catholic priest, Father David James, working in a parish in one of our cities. This is what one of my days is like.

My working day usually begins about 8.00 am. By then I would have got up and already said some prayers from the Daily Office, a special book used by priests and others. Then I go to the local parish church where I celebrate Mass, usually with just a small group on weekdays. Mass is the sacred meal of bread and wine which recalls the death and resurrection of Jesus. On weekdays the Mass is fairly relaxed and I invite the group to come up and do the readings from the Bible. Then we quietly sit down and discuss what they mean to us. On Sundays Mass is much more formal. There is a choir and I give a sermon, explaining the readings and what I see their meaning to be.

Most mornings I visit the sick people in my parish. There is a hospital not far away and I receive a list of all the Catholics who have been admitted. Other priests and ministers also go there. There's an Anglican priest, a Uniting Church minister, a Baptist minister and also a rabbi. Sometimes the patients want a simple chat. At other times they ask to receive communion, the bread that has been consecrated at the Mass. If they are very ill I may anoint them with sacred oil and say special prayers, asking God that they might be strengthened in their suffering.

The afternoon arrives quickly. After some lunch I call into the local Catholic school. I try to keep contact with the students there. Sometimes I take a class and discuss issues like war, racism or marriage. I want the students to feel that I am their friend.

On Sundays I have the morning Masses in the church and also baptisms. Baptism is the pouring of water on the head of a child to show that the child now belongs to the Church. It is a happy time with babies crying, proud parents and sometimes little brothers and sisters running around. I have to make myself heard over the noise.

It's evening. Quite often at night I have counseling, talking to people who have special problems. One person might be an alcoholic, unable to cope with alcoholic drink, and causing pain to a whole family. What can be done? A young man and woman may be having problems as they get used to living together as a married couple. There is a lot of adjustment needed in a marriage. Perhaps the man wants to be out frequently with his friends; she may be lonely. Can they learn to meet halfway? Sometimes people ask if they can come to learn about the Catholic way of life.

I'm always grateful to get to bed. I like to spend the last hour or so praying or reading quietly. I need that time of peace.

● *Working by yourself describe in a short paragraph when the rabbi is i) a preacher and ii) a healer.*

● *In another short paragraph describe when the Catholic priest is i) a preacher and ii) a healer.*

● *In your class group share your answers.*

Galilee

We are very soon going to read about Jesus who went about preaching and healing in Galilee. Galilee? Where's that? Some years ago I took my wife and two young children to live in Israel and we visited Galilee. Luckily I kept a diary like the rabbi and the priest did. It will give you some idea of what Galilee is like.

Use the map of Galilee and follow our travels.

THE LAND OF ISRAEL at the time of Jesus

SUNDAY 28 JUNE

This morning we left our apartment in Jerusalem and travelled by bus to Tiberias in Galilee. As the bus drove through the Judean hills we could see how dry and barren everything was. The heat and dust came right into the bus. However, when we reached Galilee a couple of hours later there was more greenery. But we were so thirsty!

We got off the bus in Tiberias. We had booked into a guesthouse run by the Church of Scotland. It is a very old building but the walls are thick and it was cool enough inside.

We had a short rest and went for a walk around Tiberias. It had been built by Herod Antipas, the son of the cruel Herod of the gospels. Jesus had once called Herod Antipas 'a fox', so he could not have been much better than his father. He built this city with a palace for himself in the center and a large synagogue for the Jews. There was also a stadium for games. He named the city after the Roman emperor, Tiberius. Later, many rabbis came to Tiberias to live and study. We saw the graves of some of the famous rabbis.

Since sunset it had become much cooler. We wandered down to the seafront. There were several restaurants looking over the Sea of Galilee. We chose one and had a wonderful meal of 'St Peter's fish', a special type of fish only found in this sea and named after Peter the fisherman. Salad, bread and wine went with the fish.

We were all very tired by the time we got back to the guesthouse.

Part of an ancient synagogue which has been excavated at Capernaum, on the shores of the Sea of Galilee.

MONDAY 29 JUNE

After a refreshing breakfast we went out and hired a taxi. It was old and rather uncomfortable but it was very cheap. We had to bargain with the driver to take us right around the Sea of Galilee at the right price.

Our first stop was at Tabgha. Christian pilgrims have been coming to Tabgha since the fourth century because they believe that Jesus worked the miracle of the loaves and fishes at this very spot just on the edge of the Sea of Galilee. I would have my doubts about that but the floor of an ancient church has a magnificent mosaic with a basket of bread with two fish beside it.

We returned to our friendly taxidriver and set out for Capernaum. It was midday when we arrived. Here we saw archaeology in action. Archaeology is the study of ancient civilisations. They were actually digging on the site of the old town. Capernaum is so small, only a few streets. Yet, this was where Jesus set up his headquarters in Galilee. Most of the houses must have been very small and poor and the only building of any size was the synagogue.

There is still a synagogue standing. It has beautiful stonework with carvings of grapes, figs, olives, palm trees, lions and a seven-branched candlestick which the Jews call a *menorah*. This would not have been the synagogue which Jesus attended during his days in Capernaum. It was built centuries after Jesus died but it would have been built on the very same spot as the one attended by Jesus.

Detail of the fine decorations on columns of the synagogue at Capernaum.

One house in Capernaum stood out. In fact we saw three archaeologists digging with trowels inside it. A large church had once been built over the top of this house so it must have been regarded as important. The archaeologists are fairly sure it was Peter's house where Jesus lived while he was in Capernaum.

The sun was ferocious. Miriam, our two-year-old daughter, needed plenty to drink and had to be protected from the heat.

Next our taxi took us to the Mount of Beatitudes. A beautiful round chapel was built here in 1937. It recalls Jesus speaking to his disciples about what the Christian should be like:

Happy are the poor in spirit...
Happy are the gentle...
Happy are the merciful...
Happy are the peacemakers...

From the front of this church there is a superb view over the Sea of Galilee. A Franciscan nun invited us to come in and have some iced water. It was very welcome.

We drove back to Tiberias, paid the driver and said a cheery goodbye. We had got on well with him.

TUESDAY 30 JUNE

Once more today there was a tasty breakfast. Here in Israel people have salad for breakfast. We went into the street and found a *sherut* which is a stretched taxi, like a stretch limo. It holds about eight people and was bound for Nazareth. We drove across the plain of Esdraelon and soon came to the outskirts of Nazareth.

Today Nazareth is a fairly large town and most of the people who live there are Arabs. Some of the Arabs are Christians and perhaps half are Muslim. They all regard living in Nazareth where Jesus was brought up, as a privilege. However, in Jesus' day Nazareth would have been only a small farming village with about 1600 people.

We got out of the *sherut* and found the Basilica of the Annunciation. It is really huge and very modern. It has been built over the house which is believed to have been Mary's home. The ruins of the house are at the very bottom of the basilica. Many Christians believe that it was while in this house Mary was visited by an angel and told that she would be the mother of the Messiah.

There are other churches in Nazareth. There is the Church of St Joseph and a Greek Christian church called the Church of St Mary's Well. There really is a well inside and the Greek Christians maintain that it was here that Mary received the news that she would be the mother of the Messiah. We can take our pick between the Basilica and the Well.

The children were very tired. We came back to the market and stopped at a little shop to buy lemonade. The storekeeper was very friendly and had a chat with us. He was a Christian Arab and has lived all his life in Nazareth.

By later afternoon it was difficult to find a *sherut* bound for Tiberias. When we did the driver wanted us to pay full fare for the two children even though they had to sit on our laps! We said we would get out. He gave in and let them travel free.

We had a quiet dinner in a little cafe in Tiberias.

WEDNESDAY 1 JULY

Very sadly we said goodbye to Tiberias today and boarded the bus. The children slept most of the way. The outlines of Jerusalem appeared as we came over the hills. Soon we were back again in our apartment.

(Over page; The church on the Mount of Beatitudes in the rolling hills that overlook the Sea of Gaililee.

● *Use the map and mark out my family's movements as we went from Jerusalem to Galilee and then travelled around Galilee. How far is it from Jerusalem to Tiberias, from Nazareth to Capernaum?*

● *If I were to take you with me to Galilee, which town would you like to visit most? Tell me why in a short paragraph. Share your paragraphs with others in the class.*

Jesus preaches and heals

By now you should be more familiar with some of the areas and towns in Israel. You should be able to point out Jerusalem, Galilee, Capernaum and Nazareth. You should also have some ideas about people who go about preaching and healing. Now we'll look once more at the gospels. They tell us some stories about Jesus' preaching and healing.

THE CASTING OUT OF A DEMON

Jesus and his disciples entered Capernaum. On the Sabbath Jesus taught in the synagogue. The people were quite astonished at what he was teaching. He taught with great forcefulness and not like the Jewish teachers.

There was a man who had a demon inside him in the synagogue. He yelled out, 'What do you want with us, Jesus of Nazareth? Have you come to wipe us out? We know who you are! You are God's Holy One!'

Jesus spoke sharply to him: 'Shut up! Get out of this person!' The demon made the man shake violently and then flew out of him with a loud shout. Everyone was so shocked at all of this that they started asking each other, 'What's going on? Is he teaching something new? He speaks with great power. When he gives orders even the demons obey him!'

The news of what had happened spread very rapidly. Soon Jesus was the talk of all Galilee.

No doubt you noticed where all this took place—little Capernaum. Galilee was alive with news about Jesus. When the Jews of those times looked around their world they said that Evil had taken it over. Evil was everywhere. They depicted Evil in the form of demons who crept around in the desert or hid in seas and lakes. Demons could even get inside people and make them speak and act in terrible ways.

When Mark wanted to show Jesus as the Messiah he pictured him fighting against these demons. The demons realized that the end was coming for them. They were very much afraid.

A HEALING STORY

After some days Jesus returned to Capernaum. The news soon spread that he had come back. Many people gathered and there was not enough room for them even to stand in front of the house door.

Jesus started to preach to them. Meanwhile four people carried a paralyzed man to him but because of the crowd they could not get close enough. So, they started breaking through the roof of the house where Jesus was and, when they had opened up a hole in it, they let down the stretcher on which the paralyzed man was lying. When Jesus saw how strongly they believed in him he spoke to the paralyzed man, 'Son, your sins are now forgiven.'

Some Jewish lawyers were sitting on the side and they thought to themselves, 'How come this man speaks in such a way? He is really saying dreadful things. Who can forgive sins apart from God?' Actually, Jesus knew at once inside himself what they were thinking to themselves. He said to them, 'Why are you thinking like this? What's easier— to say to this paralyzed man "Your sins are forgiven" or to say "Stand up, pick up your stretcher and walk away"? But I'll actually prove to you that I have power down here on earth to forgive sins.' Jesus now spoke to the paralyzed man, 'I tell you to get up, pick up your stretcher and go off home.'

The man did get up and straightaway he picked up his stretcher and went out while everyone was watching. They were astonished and they praised God. 'We've never seen anything like this!' they said.

The flat-roofed houses in this village are ideal places to catch the evening breezes in summer. It was down through a house like one of these that the paralyzed man was lowered.

● *In the gospel story above, try to find these parts of a miracle story:*
  - *the sad state of the man*
  - *the words or actions of Jesus*
  - *the reaction of the crowd*

● *Write each of these down. Then, in cartoon form, include each of the three in a description of the miracle.*

You have just read one of the miracle stories. There are quite a number of them in the gospels. Usually a miracle story tells us how badly off the person is who comes to Jesus. Then Jesus either speaks to such a person or performs some action. The person is wondrously cured. Then the reaction of the crowd is recorded.

The Jews were quite sure there was Evil in the world. Evil, they believed, was caused by the wrongdoing of people. But Evil also affected people's lives and bodies. The Messiah was expected to overthrow Evil. Mark shows us Jesus doing exactly that. Mark claims that Jesus is the Messiah who had come to fight Evil and eventually will overcome it.

A PARABLE

On one occasion Jesus said, 'This is what the Kingdom of God is like. A person scatters seed over the ground. As usual he sleeps at night and gets up out of bed ready for the day. All the while that seed has been sprouting and growing. The person doesn't really know how it all happens. The soil by itself produces first the blade, then the ear and finally the fully grown corn. As soon as the crop is ripe the person starts cutting it because the harvest-time has arrived.'

Jesus not only fought against evil demons and cured illnesses. He also taught people. People's minds were often mixed up by the powers of Evil and he needed to make things much clearer. For this reason he sometimes used parables.

Parables are simple stories that have a deep message in them. Jesus wanted to tell the people, more than anything else, that God had begun to rule on earth. That's what the arrival of the Kingdom of God is all about. Yet how could he explain that nothing seemed very different, that life seemed to go on as before? He used a parable.

The Kingdom of God, he said, was like the seed that the farmer sows. You can hardly see anything happening. But it is certainly growing. Soon it will grow into something quite wonderful. God, Jesus tells them, has begun something important with his own preaching and good works. It will one day reach its final point when the world will be renewed and become a place of freedom, peace and joy. God will then rule the earth. The Kingdom of God will have dawned.

JESUS IS REJECTED

(Opposite) A field of wheat in Galilee illustrates the rich harvest that Jesus spoke of in his parables.

Jesus left the shore of the Sea of Galilee and went to his own home town, Nazareth. His disciples followed him. When the Sabbath came, he taught in the synagogue. A large group listened to him. They were amazed and said things such as, 'Where did he get these ideas from?' and 'How did he become so clever?' and 'How does he do such

wonderful things?' But they also said, 'Isn't this the local carpenter, the son of Mary and brother of James, Joset, Jude and Simon? Aren't his sisters somewhere around?'

They would not accept him. Jesus said to them, 'A prophet is held in high respect everywhere except in his own home town, among his own relatives and family.' He just could not do anything marvelous there except for curing some sick people by laying hands on them. He was offended that they did not believe in him.

The Jews were expecting the Messiah to come. But they were expecting a great leader who would defeat the Romans. Jesus was well known in Galilee. He had been the local carpenter in Nazareth. Even though Jesus taught the people, cured some of their sick friends, cast out demons, he was still not accepted. They did not believe that he was the Messiah. Mark's gospel, with great sadness, tells us that Jesus was not accepted by the people closest to him.

Jesus' work continues

Jesus came as the Messiah. He came to fight against Evil. Some people rejected him. Others accepted him. He is still accepted by some and they try to continue his work. They continue to fight against evil. Let's see how the work is continued today. We asked some Christian groups, who of course accept Jesus as the Messiah or Christ, what they offer those who come to them. Here are some of their replies.

ST SAVIOUR'S ANGLICAN CHURCH

On Sundays we have an early morning service which consists of prayers and hymns with a sermon. We particularly remember those who are sick and suffering. Later in the morning, we have Holy Communion. The vicar blesses the bread and the wine and then distributes it among the people present. We recall the great things Jesus did in his lifetime.

On Sunday night we have Evensong, a beautiful collection of prayers, hymns and psalms accompanied by the organ. During the week a group of women from the parish visit an old people's home and talk particularly to the lonely ones. We distribute food and clothing to some poor families. The vicar is available for people who are in need.

ASSEMBLIES OF GOD CHURCH

We have Bible studies most mornings of the week for those who can attend. A lot of people come to discuss the Bible and see how it should affect their lives. There are several pastors available for helping people and for what is called *deliverance*. When some people realize that their lives are a real mess and that Satan, the father of all evil, has taken control, then it is possible for his power to be destroyed. There is a special deliverance ceremony to indicate that this has taken place.

Sundays are our special day. We have three main services. They consist of a sermon, prayers and Bible readings. People also have the opportunity to talk in the Spirit of God. God's spirit takes over and speaks through some believers. We call this 'talking in tongues'. During our services people who are ill are brought to the front and the pastor places his hands on them and begs God to bring them healing. Often healing does take place: blind people have been able to see, some crippled people have walked out of the church. God is wonderful in all his ways.

ST MARY'S CATHOLIC CHURCH

Our church offers people a place where they can meet to find God through Jesus. Every Sunday there are several Masses. The Mass enables people to share in the death and resurrection of Jesus. The priest consecrates the bread and wine as Jesus did at the Last Supper. Then the people share a meal together. This is accompanied by readings from the Bible and prayers.

At times people also recognize that they are sinful. They go to the church for the sacrament of reconciliation. They confess their sins to the priest and receive God's forgiveness. They feel they are in a better relationship with God and with each other.

Our church, with its two priests in charge assisted by a nun and several others, is a peaceful place in the world of today. It is a place to go when people who think like us want to meet; it is a place to go when people are in need.

• *In the gospel readings we saw Evil depicted as a demon. Write down how you would depict Evil in our world today. Perhaps you could do it in words or perhaps by means of a drawing.*

• *In the gospel reading we saw Jesus cast out demons, cure the sick and teach by explaining the Bible and telling parables. How do the followers of Jesus do each of these things today? Use the statements of the churches above to help you present your answer.*

JESUS FEEDS HIS PEOPLE

The Children of Israel, God's People, were once slaves in Egypt. Moses, their leader, saved them from this slavery. He led them out from Egypt. The leading out of Egypt is called the Exodus, which simply means an 'exit'. Jewish people have ever since rejoiced because of the Exodus. They have a particular festival for this rejoicing which is called Pesach or Passover. We are now going to look at some of the more important parts of this Passover ceremony.

The table is prepared for the Passover Meal.

(Previous page) The father of the household leads the prayers and readings during the Passover celebration in a Jewish family.

The Passover

The Passover ceremony does not take place in the synagogue but at home. This recalls the time when the Hebrew families, in the time of Moses, stood ready at night to flee from their oppression in Egypt. It is celebrated on the fourteenth day of Nisan, one of the Jewish months. This is some time around March or April.

The home table is prepared carefully. There are candles, a wine cup for each person, bowls of water with salt added, special unleavened bread called *matzah*, which does not have any yeast, and greens such as lettuce, *maror* (usually horseradish), *haroset* (a mixture of apple, nuts, cinnamon, sugar and red wine). There is a special plate on which are placed the shank bone of a lamb that has been cooked for the ceremony, some of the lettuce, some *haroset*, some *maror*.

A STORY TOLD FOR ALL PEOPLES

A leader first explains what the ceremony is about:

Now in the presence of loved ones and friends,
before us the emblems of festive rejoicing,
we gather for our sacred celebration.
With the household of Israel, our elders and young ones,
linking and bonding the past with the future,
we heed once again the divine call
to service.
Living our story that is told for all peoples,
whose shining conclusion is yet to unfold,
we gather to observe the Passover,
as it is written:

You shall keep the Feast of Unleavened Bread, for on this very day I brought your hosts out of Egypt. You shall observe this day throughout the generations for a practice for all times.

Then follows the lighting of the candles. The accompanying prayer goes like this:

In praising God we say that all life is sacred.
In kindling festive lights,
we preserve life's sanctity.
With every holy light we kindle,
the world is brightened to a higher harmony.
We praise You, God, majestic sovereign of all life,
Who hallows our lives with commandments
and bids us kindle festive holy light.

The whole family has gathered to celebrate Passover.

A first cup of wine is poured for everyone at the table. The leader begins:

> Our story tells that in diverse ways, with different words, God gave promises of freedom to our people. With cups of wine we recall each one of them as now, the first:

Everyone then says:

> I am the Lord, and I will free you from the burdens of the Egyptians.

The leader then continues:

> We take up the Kiddush cup and proclaim the holiness of this Day of Deliverance.

Then everyone takes some of the lettuce, dips it in the salty water and holds it up. This is to remind them of the bitter days their ancestors spent in Egypt. They all say:

> Praised are you, O Lord our God, King of the Universe,
> Who creates the fruit of the earth.

The lettuce is eaten and the unleavened bread is brought to the table. Everyone says:

This is the bread of affliction,
the poor bread,
which our fathers ate in the land of Egypt.
Let all who are hungry come and eat.
Let all who are in want
share the hope of Passover.
As we celebrate here,
we join with our people everywhere.
This year we celebrate here.
Next year in the land of Israel.
Now we are all still bondmen.
Next year may all be free.

WHY IS THIS NIGHT DIFFERENT?

A second cup of wine is poured for everyone and then the youngest
child who can read asks four important questions, one after the other,
without receiving a reply at once.

Why is this night different from all the other nights?
On all other nights, we eat either leavened bread or matzah;
on this night—only matzah.
On all other nights, we eat all kinds of herbs;
on this night, we especially eat bitter herbs.
On all other nights, we do not dip herbs at all;
on this night we dip them twice.
On all other nights, we eat in an ordinary manner;
tonight we dine with special ceremony.

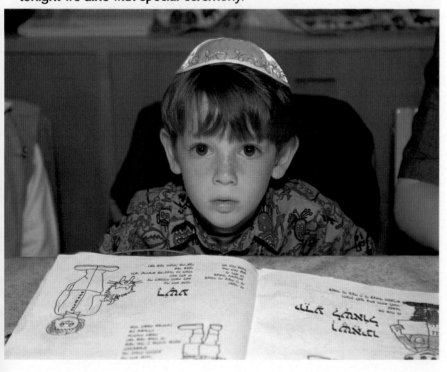

*'Why is this night different
from all the other nights?'*

The leader gives an answer to these questions:

There are many questions. Now we begin to answer.

OUR HISTORY MOVES FROM SLAVERY TOWARD FREEDOM.
OUR NARRATION BEGINS WITH DEGRADATION AND RISES
    TO DIGNITY.
OUR SERVICE OPENS WITH THE RULE OF EVIL,
AND ADVANCES TOWARD THE KINGDOM OF GOD.

'The Lord freed us from Egypt.'

This is our theme:

All join in at this point:

We were slaves to Pharaoh in Egypt, and the Lord freed us from Egypt with a mighty hand. Had not the Holy One, praised be He, delivered our people from Egypt, then we, our children, and our children's children would still be enslaved.

The leader takes up the story:

Therefore, even if
    all of us were wise,
    all of us people of understanding,
    all of us learned in Torah,
it would still be our obligation to tell the story of the Exodus from Egypt. Moreover, whoever searches deeply into its meaning is considered praiseworthy.

THE PASCHAL LAMB

Other prayers are said and then three of the symbols of Passover are discussed: the Paschal lamb, the unleavened bread and the bitter herbs.

It is explained that the roasted shank bone is a symbol of the ancient Passover sacrifice of a lamb which took place in Egypt before the Israelites left the land of the Pharaoh. The unleavened bread recalls the fact that the Children of Israel had to leave the land of Egypt so quickly that they took unleavened cakes of dough with them since they could not wait for the yeast to rise in the dough. The bitter herbs are a reminder of the bitterness of their slavery in Egypt.

A second cup of wine is now taken. The leader says:

With this second cup of wine we recall the second promise of liberation:

All join in:

As it is written: 'I will deliver you from their bondage...'
Remembering with gratitude the redemption of our fathers from Egypt,
rejoicing in the fruits of our struggle for freedom,
we look now with hope to the celebration of a future redemption,
the building of the City of Peace in which all people will rejoice
in the service of God, singing together a new song,
We praise you, O God, Redeemer of Israel!
We praise You, O God, Sovereign of all existence,
who creates the fruit of the vine!

They all drink the second cup of wine and the meal is served. At the end of the meal a third cup of wine is poured and drunk. The celebrating group then recalls Elijah. Elijah was a prophet in ancient times who helped those in need and cured the sick. When it came time for him to die, he was seen being carried to the skies in a fiery chariot. It has been a Jewish belief that Elijah would return to earth before the Messiah came. At each Passover a place is set for Elijah and the door is opened for him to enter. The group prays:

> May the All Merciful send us Elijah the Prophet to comfort us with tidings of deliverance.

NEXT YEAR IN JERUSALEM

Songs from the book of Psalms are recited and also prayers to conclude the meal.

Another cup of wine is drunk. Then the celebration is brought to its conclusion. The leader begins the final statement:

> THE SEDER SERVICE NOW CONCLUDES
> ITS RITES OBSERVED IN FULL,
> ITS PURPOSES REVEALED.

The family replies:

> THIS PRIVILEGE WE SHARE WILL EVER BE RENEWED.
> UNTIL GOD'S PLAN IS KNOWN IN FULL,
> HIS HIGHEST BLESSING SEALED.

The leader simply says: PEACE

And all reply: PEACE FOR US! FOR EVERYONE!

Leader: FOR ALL PEOPLE, THIS, OUR HOPE:

(Opposite) 'Next year in Jerusalem.'

Everyone: NEXT YEAR IN JERUSALEM!
NEXT YEAR, MAY ALL BE FREE!

The Exodus

The Passover ceremony recalls the Exodus out of Egypt. The Exodus is very important to every Jew, today and even back in the time of Jesus. I'm sure you must have a number of questions to ask after having read the Passover ceremony. Here are a few important ones:

Why do Jews eat unleavened bread at Passover?

What is so special about roast lamb?

Why do the Jews want to celebrate the ceremony in Jerusalem?

I have asked a rabbi who lives in England to describe for you what the Exodus is all about. If you listen carefully you'll find the answer to these questions. Remember that this rabbi is going to tell you the sacred story of his people. Is it true in the same way as your history books are true? We'll probably never know. But that doesn't matter. What matters is that this wonderful story lives on in the mind of every Jew. So let's give a welcome to Rabbi Michael Levi who works for the Jewish people in Manchester.

LONG AGO

I am very pleased to have this opportunity to talk about the Exodus. Long ago my people went down to Egypt. The father of the people at that time was Jacob, an old man. His son, Joseph, had been taken down there earlier as a prisoner and he became famous and a friend of the pharaoh, the king. When famine came and the people were hungry they all went down and the Egyptians were very kind. The people of Israel settled down and they worked hard.

Joseph died and the pharaohs who followed his time did not remember him. They were suspicious of the people of Israel. Perhaps this people might rise up against them and take over the throne of Egypt! So they made them slaves and forced them to build towns on the outskirts of the land. They ordered all male Israelites to be killed at birth.

One of those who escaped death at birth was Moses. He was set adrift in the river in a handmade boat. A royal princess found him and brought him up. When he became a man he realized that he must lead his people to freedom. He asked the pharaoh to free the people and let them return to their own land. The pharaoh refused. God sent dreadful punishments or plagues: the rivers turned to blood; there were plagues of frogs, gnats, flies; there was cattle disease. People were afflicted with boils and sores. The land was almost destroyed by hail and fire and locusts. A fearful darkness covered the whole land. Still the pharaoh would not allow the Israelites to go free.

Finally God ordered all the Israelite families to sacrifice a lamb and to put the blood of the lamb on the outside of their houses. Then an angel went through the land and killed the first-born child in every house where the blood was not to be seen. The angel passed over the houses of the Israelites.

The pharaoh lost his eldest son and in his grief he told the Israelites to leave. They left in such haste they did not even allow their bread to rise. They took flat bread, without yeast (unleavened bread) with them. With Moses at their head they were guided by a pillar of Fire and a Cloud. When they came to the Sea of Reeds, God made the waters divide and they went through as if it were dry land. The Egyptians had by this time decided that they wanted their slaves back. They followed, but when they got to the Sea of Reeds, the waters rolled back on them and their chariots. They were destroyed.

For forty years the Israelites wandered through the desert. God fed them with a special bread which fell like dew every morning. He provided them with water too. Despite all his care they were not always faithful and even Moses sometimes doubted God's word. After so many years God led them to the edge of the promised land. There Moses died. Because he had doubted God he was not allowed to enter the land. The people, led now by Joshua, gathered at the river Jordan and once more the waters parted. They entered the land.

The land became theirs after many battles. Later under King David they made their capital in Jerusalem and it became their holy city. When they wanted to celebrate the great things that God had done for them it was particularly in Jerusalem that such celebrations took place.

● *Let's see if you can answer those questions now. You will need to read over what Rabbi Levi has said and what was in the Passover service. Together with each answer do an illustration. Draw some pieces of* matzah *on a plate with the first answer, the roasted lamb with the second and a group of Jewish people celebrating the Passover with the third. Here are the questions again:*

● *Why do Jews eat* matzah *at Passover?*

● *What is special about roast lamb?*

● *What is so special about celebrating the Passover in Jerusalem?*

A message in numbers

Now that you know something about Moses, the Exodus out of Egypt the journey through the desert, and the Passover ceremony you are ready for some very important readings from Mark's gospel. You will need to keep your mind alert to see what the stories are about and how they connect with what we have read already.

JESUS FEEDS 5000

The apostles came back to Jesus and told him all they had been doing and what they had been teaching. He said to them: 'You need to come out to the desert alone and rest.' Many people were coming and going and the apostles did not even have time to eat. They all set off in a boat and made for the desert to be alone.

Notice first of all that Jesus is taking them to a desert. What sort of memory would a 'desert' have brought to a Jew who was reading this story?

> People saw them leave and many people could easily guess where they were heading. They hurried on foot from all the towns and were already there when the boat arrived. Jesus came ashore and saw a large crowd gathered. He was sorry for them because they were like sheep without their shepherd. He decided to teach them.

Jesus is obviously going to teach them something very important. You remember that he had been going around Galilee teaching, preaching, curing the sick and casting out demons. People did not understand what was going on. Now he is going to make things clearer. You will need to read the next section very carefully.

> It was getting very late and the disciples came to Jesus and said, 'This is a desert area and it is getting late. Send the people away to the nearby farms and villages so they can buy themselves something to eat.' Jesus said, 'It's up to you to feed them!' They replied, 'We would need to spend hundreds of dollars to get enough bread for them.' Jesus asked, 'How many loaves of bread have you got? Go and find out.' When they had done a count they said, 'Five loaves and there are two fish.' He then ordered the disciples to get the people to sit in groups on the green grass. They sat on the ground in groups of hundreds and fifties.
>
> Jesus now took the five loaves of bread and the two fish. He looked up to God and asked him to bless the loaves and fish. He then broke the loaves up and gave them to the disciples to hand out among the people. He also shared out the two fish among all of them. They all ate just as much as they wanted. The disciples went around and gathered up twelve basketfuls of bread scraps and left-over fish. Five thousand people had eaten the loaves.

You must have noticed what was happening. Out in the desert Jesus asks his Father to provide bread for a hungry people who do not understand him. Who is Jesus? He is the Messiah, the new Moses who has come to lead the people living in slavery once more. Remember the numbers in the story—five loaves, twelve basketfuls of scraps, five thousand people. Five and twelve.

The next story takes place a short time later and is very similar.

JESUS FEEDS 4000

> On another occasion a great crowd came together. They had nothing to eat. Jesus called his disciples together and said to them: 'I feel sorry for all these people. They've been with me now for three days and they have had nothing to eat. If I send them home they will collapse with hunger on

their way. Some have traveled a very long distance.' His disciples replied: 'Where could anyone possibly get sufficient bread to feed these people in a desert like this?'

Notice how similar the story is to the first one. The gospel writer wants you to take note of that. The people are again in a desert, there is no bread, Jesus had mercy on them.

Jesus asked them, 'How many loaves of bread do you have?' They said, 'Seven loaves'. He ordered the crowd to sit down on the ground and he took the seven loaves, asked God's blessing on them and broke them up and handed the pieces to the disciples to share out. They handed them out among the crowd. They also had some little fish. He asked God's blessing over these too and ordered that they should be handed out. The people ate just as much as they wanted. The disciples gathered up seven basketfuls of scraps that had been left over. There had been four thousand people.

No doubt you are sure that you've heard the whole story before. The only real change is in the numbers. Check the numbers of loaves in the two stories, the numbers of people, the numbers of basketfuls of scraps.

Nowadays we don't usually hand on messages by numbers. Numbers are for maths and calculations. But the Jews did use numbers for messages. The main message is clear: Jesus is the Messiah, the new Moses.

In the first story, the numbers are five and twelve; in the second story the numbers are four and seven. Five and twelve are very special Jewish numbers. The Bible begins with the Five Books of Moses; there were Twelve Tribes that made up Israel. Jesus, the numbers are telling us, was the Messiah of the Jews, the Messiah of Israel. Four and seven were numbers that meant the whole world, everything and everyone. There were four ends of the earth; seven was the number of perfection. And the message? Jesus is not only the Messiah of Israel (five and twelve), he is the Messiah of the whole world (four and seven). We wouldn't write like that today but it is a very clever way to write.

Many people are Christian

We have learned that Jesus came as the Messiah, the new Moses to deliver his people from their suffering. He led the first group. He went ahead and he 'passed over' from death to new life, from slavery to freedom.

Christians are those who follow Jesus, who believe that he is the Messiah and who follow the path that he has laid down. The feeding stories we have read tell us that there are many people included in the Christian world. In fact it has been estimated that at the present moment there are 1540 million Christians. They come from all nationalities, they are of all colors—white, brown, black, yellow—they speak all sorts of languages. Some are rich and some are poor.

Let us look at some of the different groups in the world who make up the Christian Church.

There are Roman Catholics. These are Christians who accept the Bishop of Rome, also known as the Pope, as their spiritual leader. They see him as the successor to Peter and the one who acts in place of Jesus. Catholics meet together on a Sunday for a sacred meal of bread and wine which they call the Mass or the Eucharist. Those who wish to belong to the Catholic Church go through a ceremony of baptism in which they have water poured over their head. They have priests who preside at the Mass. Priests also have the power to declare forgiven those who are sorry for their sins. Once, many years ago, Catholics all over the world used the Latin language when they met for prayer. Nowadays they use the language of the place where they meet although at times some Latin remains. There are some other differ-

The Greek Orthodox Patriarch of Jerusalem leads the procession on Easter Sunday in Jerusalem.

ences from country to country. Italian Catholics have special saints whom they honour; Irish Catholics have others. We have seen in chapter 2 how the feast of Christmas is celebrated in different ways in different countries.

Another large group are the Greek Orthodox. They too are Christians although they have never accepted that the Pope was the head of Christianity. Their church services are in an ancient form of Greek. Only Greek people usually belong to the Greek Orthodox Church. When Greeks go to live in another country they take their Greek Orthodox religion with them. A special place in their churches is given to *icons* (which means 'likeness'). Icons are paintings of Jesus, the Virgin Mary or holy people.

Very similar to the Greek Orthodox are the Russian Orthodox and the Syrian Orthodox. Another group who are something like these are the Copts. The Coptic Church was founded in Egypt in the early days of Christianity. They use an ancient language, which is called Coptic. It is related to the language of the ancient Egyptians.

Then there are the Protestants. Protestant churches were formed when some Catholics broke away from the Pope in the sixteenth century. Different groups formed. You may have heard of some of them: Anglicans, Lutherans, Baptists, Methodists, Presbyterians, Congregationalists. In Australia the Methodists, the Presbyterians and the Congregationalists joined together to form the Uniting Church. In the United Kingdom the main Protestant group is the Anglican Church. It is the official church in England. In the United States the Episcopalian Church is very similar to the Anglican Church. However, the United States has also many smaller breakaway church groups.

We could go on and on. There are so many different groups who could be included under the heading of 'Christian'. They differ in the languages they use, the ceremonies they perform in their churches, the customs they keep. They are united in acknowledging Jesus to be the Messiah. Most would also have at least the sacred meal of bread and wine and the baptizm of water.

● *Moses led his people in the Exodus from Egypt. Jesus led his people in a New Exodus. Start off in small groups and find out from this chapter everything you can that is similar about Jesus and Moses and everything that is similar about the Israelite Exodus and the Exodus of Jesus.*

● *Next, come together and pool all that you have found. Put all the similarities on to a chart with colours and images. Entitle the chart: JESUS AND MOSES.*

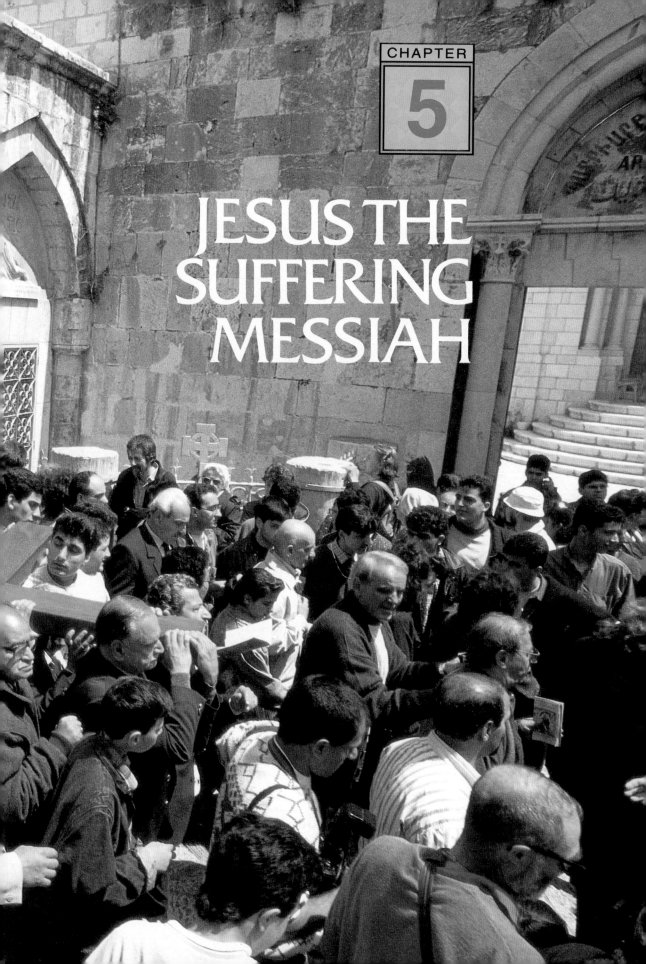

JESUS THE SUFFERING MESSIAH

esus has now shown his disciples that he is the Messiah, the one who will lead them to freedom. But he still has to teach them something that is much harder to accept. He is going to teach them that the Messiah will suffer and die. Death is not a pleasant thing to talk about. We usually try to avoid discussing death. But Jesus told his friends that he was going to die.

Tombs in the hillside below the eastern wall of the Old City.

He also told them that he would be resurrected, that he would escape from death. 'Resurrection' may be a word you are not sure about. In order to see what it means we need to do a little exercise.

(Previous page) Carrying the cross. Part of the huge crowd processing along the Way of the Cross on Good Friday in Jerusalem.

Dealing with death

We are going to have a look at the way in which people in different cultures deal with death.

HINDUISM

First we are going to see how Hindu people, who mainly live in India, face death. In one of their sacred books they have a wonderful story about a teacher who tells his young student to bring some salt and stir it up in a container of water. The student is then told to go away and return next morning. You can well imagine what had happened to the salt. It had dissolved. The water was salty. The teacher drew an important lesson from this.

Many Hindus believe that the whole world is alive. It is a big soul. Each individual person has a little soul. When we die we just mingle with the big soul. Just as salt mixes with water so we mingle with the big soul of the universe. Should we be afraid of death? 'No', say the Hindus. Death is part of living; it is a stage of life. If people live a really good life, then at death they just mingle with the great world soul. If their life was not so well lived Hindus believe they will come back again as another creature or person and they can have another try. Eventually they will reach their goal.

BUDDHISM

In Thailand when young Buddhist boys reach about fifteen they go to live in a monastery for a few months. There, they meditate. They sit quietly and they think deeply. They have to have a lot of practice. As they think they realize that there are many things they want. They want money; they want possessions; they want to be famous; they want to live a long life. All these 'I wants' are holding them back from being really happy. If they can bring themselves to get rid of all the 'I wants' then they would reach what they call Nirvana.

Sometimes Nirvana is called a 'blowing out'. It's as if all the 'I wants' and 'I needs' are blown out and they find themselves at perfect peace. That's how Buddhists face life and face death. If they do not blow out all the desires they have, then they will come back again in another form for another life. One day they will hopefully blow out all the desires and reach Nirvana.

ISLAM

Muslims, the followers of Islam, call God by the name of Allah. Allah is loving and kind. He decides everything in this world. He decides when a person will die. Muslims believe that there is not much to be gained by worrying about death. Allah already knows exactly when a person is going to die. If that person has lived a good life then a wonderful heaven has been prepared. There is joy and happiness and wonderful things that the human mind could not even imagine prepared for the good person who dies.

JUDAISM

In the old days in Israel people believed that somewhere under the earth there was a huge cave. They called it Sheol. When people died they went down to Sheol. There were good people and bad people and they more or less slept forever. Perhaps it does not seem fair that both good and bad ended up in Sheol. Some Jews would say that if you lived a good life then you would have been very happy already. You

would have been rich and would have had a lovely family. But already in the time of the Book of Job this view was challenged.

As we come down close to the time of Jesus we find that Jews were suffering a great deal. They were being persecuted, they were being punished by other nations. Young Jews were being put to death because they would not worship Greek gods instead of the God of Israel. What would happen to them? Would they go down to Sheol? Some Jews decided that God would go down to Sheol and resurrect the good people.

Cemetery outside the eastern wall of the Old City. The Dome of the Rock is visible beyond the wall.

'Resurrect' means to raise up. God, Jews believed, would pull them up out of this great cave. Then they could live in peace on a new earth. There would no longer be any suffering, there would be no death, no tears. The good ones would live forever. Although many Jews would not believe exactly this today it is important for us, trying to understand what the early Christians handed on to us, to understand the ancient belief about life beyond death.

The suffering of the Jewish people

We can see that the Jews thought differently from the other groups of people we have looked at. They also went through a great change in their thinking. Why? Because of their suffering. To them it seemed that no people probably had suffered as much as they had. Let us suppose that they had press releases in those days just as we do in our newspapers. We will make up some press releases with headlines describing the terrible things that happened to the Jewish people before Jesus arrived. We may get some idea of how much they suffered and longed for relief.

Jerusalem, 22 November 722
SAMARIA FALLS TO THE ASSYRIAN ARMY!

The northern capital, Samaria, has fallen to the fierce army of the Assyrian king, Sargon. Despite its great wealth the city was not able to withstand the enemy forces. The Assyrians had surrounded it and deprived the inhabitants of food and water. There was nothing for them to do but surrender. It is believed that the beautiful palaces with their ivory carvings have been burned. The leaders have been deported and taken to Assyria. We no longer have a neighbor in the north.

Beersheba, 15 July 587
BABYLONIANS INVADE HOLY CITY OF DAVID

It is a sad day for all Israel. After a long resistance the city of Jerusalem fell today to the Babylonians. King Nebuchadnezzar ordered his troops to break through the walls of the city. They burned the Temple of God to the ground. The Israelite king, Zedekiah, was last seen being led into exile. Together with him went the nobles and the priests of the Temple. Only peasants remain in the ruins of the city.

Somewhere in Mesopotamia, 5 October 538
CYRUS SETS ISRAELITES FREE. 'WE CAN GO HOME!'

There is great rejoicing in the Israelite camps tonight as the news spreads that Cyrus, who recently defeated the Babylonian army, has passed a decree allowing the Israelites to return to their homeland. One Israelite leader rejoiced: 'Cyrus has said that we can take back with us to Jerusalem the sacred objects stolen by the Babylonians and we can rebuild the ruined Temple. The Persians will be our masters, but they will be kinder than the Babylonians who have received what they deserved.'

(Following page) Praying at the Wall. Slips of paper with private prayers or petitions are often placed in the cracks between the stones.

The Lions' Gate leads to the cemetery outside the eastern wall of the Old City.

Alexandria, 8 December 167
GREEK SOLDIERS DEFILE THE TEMPLE OF JERUSALEM

The Greeks have taken over Jerusalem. A decree has been passed ordering all Jewish religious practices to stop at once. No Jewish child may be circumcised. No worship may be paid to their God. A statue of the Greek god Zeus has been set up in the Temple. Already sacrifice has been offered in the Temple area to Zeus. Several young Jewish men who refused to worship Zeus were condemned to death and executed.

Jerusalem, 14 July 37
HEROD MADE KING OF THE JEWS

- *Do some research on one of the oppressors of Israel. You could choose from Assyrians, Babylonians, Persians, Greeks or Romans.*

- *Draw a map showing where the oppressor came from.*

- *Show on the map where the oppressor travelled on the way to Israel.*

- *Describe the battles between Israel and the oppressor.*

- *How did the oppressor treat Israel?*

The Roman forces occupying Israelite territory have announced that Herod is to be known as King of the Jews. Ever since they took over Jewish lands in the year 63 they began to interfere in local politics. 'This is the last straw', said a spokesperson, 'Herod is an evil man. He does not deserve to be our king. He has announced that he intends to rebuild many of the cities of our land including the city of Jerusalem. He even intends to rebuild the Holy Temple!'

All these are sad headlines. The Jewish people knew oppression over a long period of time. There was one oppressor after another: Assyrians, Babylonians, Persians, Greeks and Romans. It was towards the end of the time of oppression, when the Greeks were still in charge, that some Jewish thinkers came to the realization that God would resurrect the good people who had died. They believed that he would go down to Sheol, when the world had come to an end, and he would draw up the good people. Suffering would be followed by resurrection and resurrection would mean joy and the loving presence of their God.

Jesus is to suffer and die

We now come to the very centre of the gospel of Mark. Jesus has already shown by his preaching, healing and casting out of demons that he is the Messiah. He has not been understood by the people who have seen what he has done and heard his words.

JESUS CURES A BLIND MAN

Jesus and the disciples came to Bethsaida. A blind man was brought to him and people begged Jesus to touch this man. He took the blind man by the hand and led him outside the village. He put some spittle on the man's eyes and placed his hands on him. Then he asked, 'Can you see

The Garden of Gethsemane, at the foot of the Mount of Olives, where Jesus prayed on the night of his capture.

anything yet?' The man was just beginning to see vaguely and he said, 'I can see people but they look like trees to me, trees walking around.' Jesus laid his hands on the man's eyes a second time. Now he saw quite clearly. He was cured and could see plainly and distinctly.

This is a very important healing story. No doubt you've noticed that it is different from other stories. The man is not cured at once. At first he sees things as if in a mist. Then he sees clearly. Does this remind you of anyone?

Think of Jesus' disciples. They saw Jesus as a wonderworker, kind and caring. They understood vaguely. They still did not understand

• *Take one of these prayers and explain what it means. You will need to refer to the resurrection of Jesus and the resurrection of the Christian, to the suffering of Jesus and the suffering of the Christian. Small groups could take different prayers and explain them. Then, when everyone in the class has come together a spokesperson for each group could read out the prayer and another person from the group give the group's explanation.*

• *Next you can do a project by yourself. You saw above that other religions have their explanations about death and what happens after death. In a short paragraph explain to a non-Christian how a Christian sees death and life beyond death.*

The death of a Christian should be different too. Have you ever been to a Christian funeral? Here we will look at some of the prayers that might be said at a Christian funeral.

Lord Jesus Christ,
by the three days you lay in the tomb
you made holy the graves of all who believe in you;
and even though their bodies lie in the earth,
they trust that they, like you, will rise again.

Give our brother (or sister) peaceful rest in this grave,
until that day when you, the resurrection and the life,
will raise him (or her) up in glory.
Then may he (or she) see the light of your presence,
Lord Jesus,
in the kingdom where you live for ever and ever.
Amen

Since almighty God had called our brother (or sister)
from this life to himself,
we commit his (or her) body
to the earth from which it was made.

Christ was the first to rise from the dead,
and we know that he will raise up our mortal bodies
to be like his in glory.

We commend our brother (or sister) to the Lord:
may the Lord receive him (or her) into his peace
and raise up his (or her) body on the last day.

Lord Jesus,
our Redeemer,
you willingly gave yourself up to death
so that all people might be saved
and pass from death into a new life.
Listen to our prayers,
look with love on your people
who mourn and pray for their dead brother (or sister).
Lord Jesus, you alone are holy and compassionate:
Forgive our brother (or sister) his (or her) sins.
By dying you opened the gates of life
for those who believe in you:
do not let our brother (or sister) be parted from you,
but by your glorious power
give him (or her) light, joy, and peace in heaven
where you live for ever and ever.
Amen.

JESUS IN JERUSALEM

Bringing the past into the present

- *Create a quiet atmosphere in the classroom. No talking. No moving around. Breathe slowly and calmly. Now try these exercises:*

  - Remember *one happy event from the past that really happened to you.*

  - Remember *one sad event from the past that really happened to you.*

  - Imagine *one happy event that might have happened to you.*

  - Imagine *one sad event that might have happened to you.*

Memories are really wonderful. Sometimes I find a quiet spot where I can let my mind bring back all sorts of memories. I can remember many things that happened to me so long ago. Sometimes the memories are so real that it seems that the events from the past are taking place again here and now. If the event I remember was a happy and joyous one, then once again I can feel happy just as I did the first time. If it was a sad event then once again I become downcast. My memory makes the past come back into the present.

But I have more than a memory. I also have an imagination. I have a good imagination. I can use my imagination to recall events even before I was born. I can imagine hearing the announcement that World War 1 was over, even though I was not born then. I can feel the joy and the relief. I can even imagine things that didn't happen.

I sometimes write stories and I put into them events, some happy and some sad, that never happened although they could have happened. I want the reader to imagine the event and to feel either sadness or happiness.

Of course, imagining is more difficult than remembering. Historians and archaeologists spend much time imagining. They study the past and they have to make the past live again. They use written texts which people have left behind and they use left-over bits and pieces which archaeology has uncovered.

Writing is really language, the speech which comes out of our lips. But once we've spoken some words they can be lost unless someone remembers them later. It's much easier for words to be kept if they are written down. It's easier to remember them. That's why we have shopping lists and why school reports are written. Whenever we want to keep some important idea safely, we write it down.

DISCOVERING THE PAST

(Previous page) The roof of the convent of the Sisters of Notre Dame de Sion (the Ecce Homo: 'Behold the Man') provides a magnificent view of the city of Jerusalem, especially the Dome of the Rock.

Archaeology is the study of ancient things. When people live in the same place for a long time, like hundreds or thousands of years, they leave behind many things. They build houses and even though the houses may have been destroyed the foundations still remain. People eat and they leave behind their plates and cups, often pottery ones. They even leave behind seeds from their food. They paint and they sculpt. They dig fields and they use tools. They have weapons for hunting and fighting. So we find that house foundations, walls, pottery, wall paintings, tools and weapons are often left behind.

When people have abandoned a town for many, many years the

winds blow dust, sand and rubbish among the ruins. Plants grow, rot and are replaced by more plants. Soon the soil rises around and above the ruins. After many more years all that is left is a mound of soil, with the ruins inside the mound. Archaeologists come along, find the mound and dig away the soil. They find the ruins underneath and can then imagine what the life of the people who lived there was like.

Both historians and archaeologists use their imagination. They bring the past into the present. They make the past live once more. That's why history should be so exciting. Ancient writing and archaeological finds are used as if they were memories. But why do we use memory and imagination?

Excavation at Qumran, where scrolls containing the Hebrew scriptures and other early writings were discovered.

ANNIVERSARIES

Usually we do so because a past event is important in some way. In 1989 the people of France celebrated the two hundredth anniversary of the French Revolution, which had taken place in 1789. The French Revolution meant that the people in France no longer wanted to be ruled by kings and have no say in how they lived their lives. They wanted everyone to be free and equal. The king was executed. It was the beginning of a new period of French history. It was worth remembering.

Quite clearly everyone associated with the French Revolution has been dead for a very long time. But writings from that time have come down to us: accounts of what took place, letters, decrees. These can be used to imagine what happened.

In July 1989 Paris celebrated the French Revolution. There were speeches and ceremonies. On one beautiful summer's night, hundreds of thousands of people gathered in the Place de la Concorde where the Revolution had had its centre. They sang the *Marseillaise*, the song that had inspired the first revolutionaries 200 years ago. It was as if the French Revolution were happening in 1989 and not 1789. The French Revolution was made to happen again because it was 200 years old in 1989.

Sometimes we want a past event to live again more regularly. In Australia one of the most memorable events from the past was the attack by Australian troops on the shores of Turkey on 25 April, 1915. The landing place was called Anzac Cove. Many young Australians were killed. Remembering such an event brings feelings of deep sadness but it also arouses pride in the bravery of those Australians.

Hence, every year on 25 April, the date of the landing, ceremonies take place all round Australia. Sometimes the ceremony is simple—a few words, the laying of a wreath at a war memorial. Sometimes, it is an elaborate ceremony in a cathedral. Sometimes it takes the form of a long procession through city streets with bands playing and soldiers marching. Year after year the past is brought into the present. Memory and imagination play their parts.

On 4 July the United States celebrates. It celebrates its independence from England which took place in 1776. Parades are features of most American cities on that day; there are public speeches which recall the famous Declaration of Independence. Then at night the sky is alive with fireworks. All of this is a memorial of the fact that the United States broke away from its mother country; it established itself as a new and independent nation. America remembers.

RELIGION AND MEMORY

Religions have memories too. Christianity recalls the great events of the life of Jesus, those you are studying in this book. In fact Jesus, in the

The Passover feast provides an opportunity for Jews to remember what God has done for them.

gospels, indicated how his own 'memorial' should take place.

You have already been introduced to a Jewish memorial, the Passover or Pesach. The rabbi explained that it was a memorial of the Exodus from Egypt. Jews gather together at a special time, around a family table, and they eat a special meal of unleavened bread and wine. It is as if the Exodus becomes real for them once more. It is almost as if they become members of the group who left Egypt and its slavery and march towards the new life in the land of Israel.

Jews at the time of Jesus celebrated the memorial meal of the Passover. Since Jesus was a Jew, he must have celebrated it year by year. But before he died he changed the ceremony. Eating the bread and drinking the wine had reminded the Jews that they were part of the people who had undergone the Exodus. Jesus told his disciples that eating the bread and drinking the wine was to remind them of him, of the fact that he too was to have an Exodus, that he would pass over from death to a new life with God.

That is why we call the Mass (some Christians call it Holy Communion or the Lord's Supper or the Eucharist) a memorial. It is a very important memorial or 'remembering'. It brings the past into the present. Some Christians have such a memorial service often, others less often.

● *Obtain the text used in your church for Mass or Holy Communion. Find the words which the priest or minister uses over the bread and wine. What do you understand them to mean? What part does the priest or minister play in the memorial? Whom does he or she represent?*

THE OLD CITY OF JERUSALEM

I am now going to share some memories with you which will help with the gospel readings we will look at next. Below is a map of the city of Jerusalem. You will need to follow it very closely. We will walk together through the streets of Jerusalem as they are today. Since I once lived in Jerusalem they are quite familiar to me. Come with me and share in the experience.

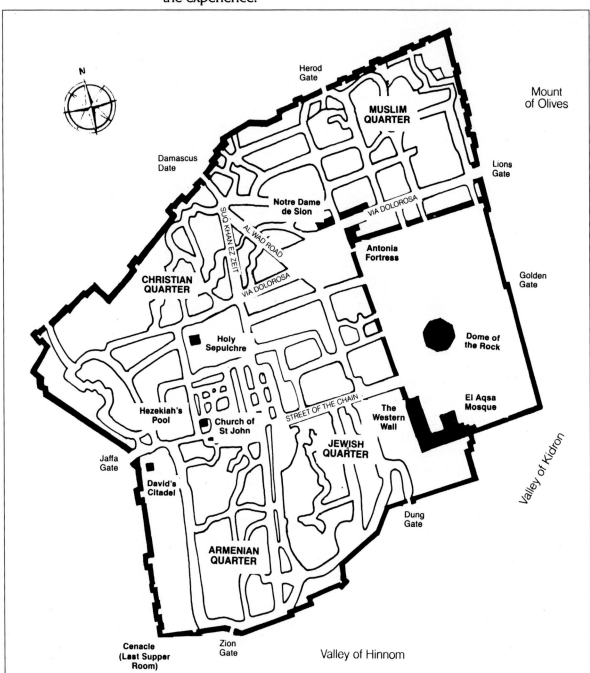

The old city of Jerusalem

(Over page) The magnificent Mosque of Omar—the Dome of the Rock. Tradition says that the rock inside the mosque was the one on which Abraham prepared to sacrifice his son Isaac.

Along the Via Dolorosa are the fourteen stations of the Cross, the last five of which are inside the Church of the Holy Sepulchre.

I'm now entering the most ancient part of Jerusalem, called the Old City, by the Damascus Gate. Can you find it on the map? As I walk through the gate it is almost as if another world appears. There are narrow streets with tiny, very old shops. People are selling all sorts of things and there are so many smells, some pleasant and some nasty. I can smell coffee and see men sitting inside a coffee shop with their cups of sweet coffee.

Very soon I come to a point where two streets branch off. I take the street to the left, Al Wad Road. It leads me to the Via Dolorosa. In Latin *Via Dolorosa* means the Street of Sorrow. It recalls the path taken by Jesus after he had been condemned to death by Pilate, the local Roman ruler, and then made to carry his cross to a mound outside the city walls called Calvary.

Just off the Via Dolorosa I find a small gateway in the wall and go through. I now see the most magnificent building, the Dome of the Rock. It belongs not to Christians, but to Muslims, the people of Islam. It is one of their most sacred places. Its golden dome glistens in the sun. Somewhere beneath this building and the platform on which it is built lies the remains of the great Temple of Jerusalem.

The Temple was the centre of Jewish worship. The first Temple was built by Solomon, son of King David. I sit down in the courtyard looking at the Dome of the Rock and remembering. Here Jesus would have come to pray; here Jesus' first disciples met. The Jews believed that their God dwelt here in a very special way.

Babylonians had destroyed the first Temple almost six hundred years before the time of Jesus. Later the Persians had allowed the Jews to rebuild a second Temple. It was extended and was still being rebuilt during the lifetime of Jesus. After Jesus' death it was destroyed by the Romans and was never replaced.

Inside the Dome of the Rock I can see the full beauty of this house of Islam. Having walked across the platform I leave the Temple area and find myself near the Western Wall. This is part of a retaining wall to close off the Temple area. The Wall has always been held in great esteem by the Jews. For them it is the last remnant of the Temple. I go up to the Wall to pray, making sure that my head is covered as a mark of respect.

Church of the Holy Sepulchre—the site of the death and resurrection of Jesus.

Leaving the Wall I make for the Church of the Holy Sepulchre. 'Sepulchre' is another word for 'tomb'. In this large and ancient church there is a memorial of the mound of Calvary, the place where Jesus was crucified. There is also a stone memorial of the tomb where he was buried. We are not absolutely sure that this was exactly where Calvary and the tomb were situated but that is not really important.

This church is very important for Christians. It is very dark inside and there is always the smell of incense. I can see some Catholic priests in brown habits, some Greek Orthodox priests in their black robes and hoods. Climbing a stairway brings me to Calvary. It is a small crowded area above the main body of the Church and there are three altars.

I leave the Church of the Holy Sepulchre and walk south. I go through the Armenian Quarter and through the Zion Gate. Outside the walls I find the Cenacle, the room where Jesus and his disciples ate the Last Supper. It is bare and nothing like you would expect. Here I remember that Jesus, while eating the Passover meal on the night before he died, changed the meaning of the memorial.

Jesus in Jerusalem

We are next going to look at some texts from Mark's gospel which recount the events in which Jesus was caught up during the last days of his life. You will need to keep the plan of Jerusalem in front of you.

JESUS' ENTRY INTO JERUSALEM

As they were now approaching Jerusalem, near Bethphage and Bethany on the Mount of Olives, Jesus sent off two of his disciples with these words, 'Go into that village over there and as soon as you get to it you will find a colt tied up. It's one that no-one has ever ridden. Untie it and bring it back to me. If anyone should ask you, "What are you doing?" just say "The Lord needs it and he'll give it back to you very soon".' So they went off.

They found a young colt tied up to a doorpost in the street. They untied it. Some people who were standing around said, 'What are you up to? Why are you untying the colt?' They answered them in the way Jesus had told them. The people let them go ahead.

They brought the colt to Jesus and then put their cloaks on it. Jesus sat on the colt. People spread some of their clothes on the roadway. Others spread green branches they had cut in the fields. The crowd walking with him kept on crying out, 'Hosanna! May God bless this person who has come to represent him! God bless the Kingdom of David which is soon to come! Hosanna in the heavens above!'

Jesus went into Jerusalem and entered the Temple.

View of the Old City from the Mount of Olives.

We know that the Jews had been waiting for the coming of the Messiah. One of their prophets had written this:

> Rejoice, rejoice, Daughter of Zion.
> Shout aloud, Daughter of Jerusalem.
> Look, look! Your King is coming to you.
> He has won what he set out to win.
> He is victorious.
> He is a humble person, sitting on an ass
> on a foal, the young of a she-ass.

This is a short poem. It was telling the Jews (calling them 'Daughter of Jerusalem', or 'Daughter of Zion' which is another word for Jerusalem) that they should look forward to their King or Messiah. He would come unexpectedly to their city. Mark is describing the entry of Jesus into Jerusalem in just that way. The people acclaim him as he goes into the city. Of course he, being a good Jew, makes for the most holy place in the city, the Temple.

The Passover and the Festival of Unleavened Bread were only two days away. The chief priests and some of the scholars were trying to think up a clever plan to seize Jesus and kill him. They were saying, 'It just cannot be done during the Festival. The people would rise up.'

While this was all going on, Jesus was in Bethany in the house of a person called Simon the Leper. While they were all sitting at the table, a woman came up to him. She was carrying a small bottle of very costly perfume, pure oil of nard. She broke the bottle open and poured the oil over his head. Some of the people were quite upset at this and they said, 'What a waste! This perfume could have been sold for hundreds of dollars!' Jesus said to them, 'Let her alone. Why are you picking on her? She has done something wonderful. You will always have the poor among you and you will always be able to lend them a hand. You won't always have me. She's done the best thing possible. She has embalmed my body ready for death. I'll tell you something else—whenever the Good News is told in any part of the world, what she has done will be remembered.'

Then Judas Iscariot, who was one of the Twelve, went off to the chief priests to arrange for Jesus to be handed over. The chief priests were delighted when they realized why he had come. They promised him some money. They were looking for the chance to get their hands on him.

JESUS PREPARES FOR HIS DEATH

Did you notice that this story has three parts? They are divided up for you. Read the first and third parts together. They tell how Jesus' enemies were planning to hand Jesus over to the Romans. Judas played right into their hands.

After so many centuries it is very difficult to decide who exactly arranged the death of Jesus. We know that it was the Romans who executed him and only they had the authority to do so. We know that Jesus was a good Jew and that most Jews would have had no reason but to look upon him as a very good person.

Later on, the Christians, including the gospel writers, tended to put more and more blame on the Jews. Christians and Jews had become enemies. However, the important point that is being made in sections one and three is that people are scheming to do away with Jesus.

But the second part of the story tells us something quite different. The two main characters are Jesus and a woman. While you may be used to women doing anything men can do, that was not true in the time of Jesus. It must have come as a shock for the early Christians to be told this story of a woman pouring oil over the head of Jesus. Why did she do it? She was anointing Jesus. Do you remember the word for an 'anointed person'? It is 'Messiah'! She is performing a very special ceremony. She is anointing the Messiah of the People of Israel.

Then Jesus points out a deeper meaning. She is not only anointing him as the Messiah, she is embalming his body. Sometimes when people die their bodies are rubbed with oil to make sure that they do not decompose too quickly. Jesus is saying that the Messiah will die. So, while other people might be plotting his death and thinking they have his death under control, Jesus is saying that his death is part of God's plan. One day it will be understood what the woman did: she anointed and embalmed the Messiah.

THE LAST SUPPER

Jesus and his disciples were eating a meal together. Jesus lifted up the bread and asked God to bless it. He broke the bread into pieces and handed them out to the disciples. He said to them: 'Take a piece. This is me.' Next he took the cup. He gave God thanks for it. Then he said: 'This is my "Blood of the Covenant". For the sake of the people it has been poured out. I will say something very serious; I will never drink wine again until I drink new wine in the Kingdom of God!'

We have already discussed memorials and also the Passover. Jesus is celebrating a Passover meal with his family, the disciples. The bread and the wine have been laid out on the table. Because they are Jews, they are recalling the Exodus out of Egypt. That is of great importance to them all. But Jesus now changes the ceremony. He makes it a memorial of his coming death and his new life.

For Jews the Passover recalled passing over from slavery in Egypt to new life in the land of Canaan. Jesus says that eating the bread and drinking the wine for Christians will recall his passing over from death to new life with God. Christians can make use of the ceremony to bring the past into the present.

Notice how Jesus says that the wine is his 'Blood of the Covenant'. When Moses was meeting with God at Mount Sinai he had oxen sacrificed and their blood collected in bowls. Some of this blood was splashed on an altar (which stood for God) and the rest was sprinkled over the people. It was as if the blood united God to the people. Moses then said: 'This is the Blood of the Covenant.' We've already met the word 'covenant'. It means a treaty, an agreement between two groups, in this case God and Israel.

The blood on Mount Sinai signified that God and the people had made an agreement. God would be the God of Israel and Israel would be the People of God. Now Jesus says that the wine of this festival will be a memorial not only of the blood shed at Sinai but also of his blood, his death for the sake of the people he loved.

The Jewish people—past and present

We are now going to start a very special assignment. You will need to work in small groups preparing a poster. You will need three headings across the top of the poster:

SUFFERING OF ISRAEL   EXODUS UNDER MOSES   NEW LIFE

Under SUFFERING OF ISRAEL write a paragraph telling of the sad times the people of Israel underwent in Egypt. You may need to look up the book of Exodus chapters 1-12 for some details. You could also draw something appropriate to go with the description.

Under EXODUS UNDER MOSES describe the main features of the Exodus out of Egypt and the journey through the desert. You will need to mention the meeting of God and Moses at Sinai. This could be accompanied by a drawing or a map. You will find all the material you need in Exodus chapters 13-19.

Under NEW LIFE describe what the People of Israel found in the land of Canaan. You could include the fact that they eventually made Jerusalem their capital city and built the Temple to the God of Israel there. You could design an illustration for this too. Information for this section will be found in Joshua chapters 1-6, 2 Samuel chapters 5-6 and 1 Kings chapters 6-8.

Finally at the bottom of the poster include a special section on the PASSOVER. Describe the celebration of the Passover and what it meant, as a memorial, to Jews, including Jesus and his followers.

JESUS DIES AND RISES

Change in our lives

(Previous page) Passing the Easter flame. Part of the crowd at the Holy Sepulchre celebrating Greek Easter. A flame from within the Sepulchre is passed among the people.

Some things go unchanged —shepherds still tend to their sheep in Israel today. Some do change, though—note this shepherd's Walkman!

In this last chapter we are going to look at changes. There are always changes that take place in people's lives. You must have had some major changes in your life already and there are certainly big changes ahead. Leaving school will be a great change. You will need to think of some occupation that will both be interesting and provide an income. Perhaps at some stage you may consider marriage. That will bring great change into your life. You may also decide to have children. Your life will change again.

We are now going to look at some drastic changes that have taken place in certain people's lives. We will also see the effect that such change had on those people.

ROGER SCHUTZ AT TAIZE

In the south of France there is a small town called Taizé. In 1940 a very remarkable man called Roger Schutz arrived in Taizé. He was the son of a Protestant minister and he had decided to start up a Christian monastery where Christians generally could share a new way of life.

The early 1940s were bad times. The whole world it seemed was at war. Roger and a few friends who joined him found themselves in a country invaded by Nazi Germany. There were Jews living in Taizé. Hitler, the Nazi leader of Germany, had decided that Jews were less than human. They had to be wiped out. Roger and his friends allowed some Jews to hide in their house and soon the house became a refuge for people fleeing from the Nazi persecution. When the Nazis closed in upon Taizé, Roger and this group had to escape to Switzerland.

However, they returned in 1944 and the next year the war ended. They now set about building their monastery in earnest. They wore everyday clothes except when they went to the chapel to pray. At such times they wore a long white robe with a hood. For the rest of the day they worked in ordinary occupations. There were teachers, doctors, printers, artists and farmers among them.

Roger and his companions maintained that coming to Taizé reflected a great change in their lives. They had come to realize something about Christianity and it had changed them. They arrived at Taizé changed people. The result of the change was visible: they had found a deep peace and a deep sharing in this little town. Yet as they looked around the world they found that even Christians were not living in peace with each other. Roger's claim was that if Christians could live together in peace at Taizé then Christians everywhere could live together peacefully.

Roger had a larger church built at Taizé. It was called the Church of the Reconciliation. 'Reconciliation' means forgiveness, forgetting the hurtful past, sharing a peaceful life together. Roger wanted Catholics, Lutherans, Anglicans, Presbyterians and all other Christians to come to Taizé and see their way of life. He was sure that if people could see how they lived in peace then they would want to share that peacefulness.

Roger and his group had undergone a change. They wanted others to change too. Roger maintained that he had been changed because of his belief in the resurrection of Jesus, his rising from the dead. If Jesus had overcome death, then, Roger believed, life for all Christians should be different. That belief led him to Taizé. He wanted others to come and see for themselves.

● *Think over what has happened to you so far in life. What were the really great changes? Some examples would be: starting school, changing schools, shifting house, the arrival of a new brother or sister, the death of a relative. Choose one major change that you are willing to talk about and prepare a class talk along the following lines:*

● *Describe the change in your life.*

● *Describe its effect upon you.*

● *Show some ways in which your life afterwards was different.*

A STORY FROM THE ACTS OF THE APOSTLES

In the second half of the Gospel of Luke, called the Acts of the Apostles, we read that the first disciples of Jesus were gathered in a house together after his death. It was at the time of the Jewish festival of Pentecost, the time when the Jews recalled that Moses met God on Mount Sinai.

There was the sound of rushing wind. Fire was seen in the shape of tongues and these tongues came down over the heads of the disciples. Both wind and fire meant much to the Jews. In their sacred language, Hebrew, 'wind' and 'spirit' were the same word. When they spoke about God doing things powerfully in the world they described him as the Spirit of Holiness which also meant the Wind of Holiness. Fire was also used as an image of God. The sound of wind and the tongues of fire meant that God was about to achieve something dramatic and powerful in the world.

Luke's text next tells us that 'they were all filled with the Spirit of God and began to talk in other languages'. The impossible had happened. The disciples could preach the message of Jesus to everyone. They were filled with the power of God just as Jesus had been. It was as if Jesus were living on in them and speaking through them. The resurrection, the continued life of Jesus after his death, had brought about a dramatic change in the disciples. They would never be the same again.

A STORY FROM JOHN'S GOSPEL

The Greek Orthodox Church of St John.

This story is taken from John's gospel. On the Sunday when the resurrection of Jesus occurred the disciples were together. They had bolted fast the doors of the room where they were staying. They were afraid that they too might be executed.

Jesus appeared among them. He said, 'May you share peace among you.' He then showed them the wounds made by the nails in his hands and the wound in his side. The disciples were quite overcome with joy.

Jesus breathed on them. 'Breath' is also another word for Spirit. Jesus was handing on to them the Spirit of God. He said: 'Receive God's Spirit'. He told them that he was sending them out into the world to bring peace and understanding among all people. They were changed so that they could do the work of Jesus. Roger Schutz was changed in the same way.

These stories show that the death and resurrection of Jesus

marked a deep change in the lives of people both in the past and in the present. We will now look at the texts in Mark's gospel that tell us about this death and resurrection.

THE DEATH OF JESUS

It was around midday. Darkness fell. It stayed like that until three o'clock in the afternoon. At three o'clock Jesus screamed, 'Eloi, Eloi, lama sabachtani.' That meant: 'My God, my God, why have you left me?' Some of those who stood by heard this. They said, 'He is calling on Elijah!' One of them went off and soaked a sponge full of sour wine. He put the sponge on the end of a stick and gave it to Jesus so he could have a drink. He said, 'Just a minute! Let's wait and see if Elijah is really going to come and rescue him.'

Jesus cried out loudly and died.

One important thing to remember about the story of Jesus' death in Mark's gospel is that Jesus is praying on the cross. Mark tells us that he was using the psalms as his prayers. The Book of Psalms is something like an ancient Jewish hymn book. One particular psalm began like this:

My God, my God, why have you left me?

Jesus would have used his own language, which was Aramaic, and Mark has left the first line in Aramaic. Those who were around the cross did not understand him. They were the Roman executioners. They thought that he was calling on Elijah when he said 'Eloi'. You remember that the Jews expected that Elijah would return to earth before the Messiah came. Perhaps the Roman soldiers wondered if something dramatic might happen.

Mark expected his readers to know the rest of the psalm and to know that Jesus, after saying the first line aloud, would continue to pray it. The psalm continues:

Why do you stand so far off when I need help?
I am more like a worm than a real person.
I have been pushed aside by people, hated by them.

This is a good description of the plight of Jesus. Its conclusion is:

Even proud people will one day worship God.
Every human being will bow down before him.
People will tell their children what God has done.
They will tell the next generation how he made them free.

This is Psalm 22. When the people of Israel sang it they were aware that in so many ways they were a good people, yet they were being punished and persecuted. They were sure that one day God would set them free. Mark sees that the psalm is very appropriate on the lips of Jesus.

There is another psalm with much the same message, Psalm 69. One important line in it reads:

They gave me poison instead of food,
when I was thirsty they gave me sour wine to drink.

That must remind you of the account of the death of Jesus. Psalm 69 also ends up on a happy note:

> God will save Jerusalem
> and he will build up Judah's towns again.
> His servants will live there peacefully.
> Their children will inherit the land.
> and whoever loves God will live in that land.

These two psalms were prayers to be used by good Jews who praised their God and sought justice from him. Mark has shown us that Jesus was good, the Messiah of the People of Israel. His suffering and death were not deserved. He should be saved. Whether Mark actually knew what Jesus said while he was on the cross does not matter. What matters is that Mark is explaining what really was taking place in his dying.

THE RESURRECTION OF JESUS

On the Saturday evening Mary Magdalene, and Mary who was James' mother, and Salome bought herbs to embalm Jesus' body. They set out for the tomb on the Sunday morning. The sun had just risen. They discussed with each other: 'Who is going to roll away the stone door of the tomb?' Then they stared and realized that the stone door was already rolled back. The stone was huge. They went inside the tomb and they saw a young man over on the right. He was dressed in white. They could not believe their eyes. He said to them, 'Don't be shocked. You're looking for Jesus of Nazareth, who was put to death on the cross. He has risen. He's no longer here. You can see where they laid out his body. Leave now and tell his disciples, particularly Peter, that he will go ahead of them into Galilee. He will meet all of you there, just as he told you he would.'

The women left the tomb and ran away quickly. They were shaking. They were frightened. They said nothing at all because they were so afraid.

The resurrection of Jesus means that he was able to overcome death. It had an unsettling effect on people, as we can see when the women found the tomb empty.

In the story, resurrection and death go together. Jesus died for other people, a good Jew who gave himself entirely for others. He had been raised from the dead as the Jews expected.

Christians claim that he was the first to be raised. That is what Mark's story is all about. Jesus did not die forever. He lived on and still lives on. He can still do the work that he began in Galilee, preaching and healing.

Jesus preaches and heals through people whose lives have been changed by his death and resurrection. The resurrection marks a great point of change in the lives of many people.

Inside the Church of the Holy Sepulchre.

The Christian people—past and present

We now come to the most important project of all. You have already completed posters with three headings:

SUFFERING OF ISRAEL

EXODUS UNDER MOSES

NEW LIFE

Now it is time to start a second poster. This one will also have three headings:

SUFFERING OF ISRAEL

NEW EXODUS UNDER JESUS

NEW LIFE

Under SUFFERING OF ISRAEL write a paragraph about the suffering the Jews underwent under the Greeks and Romans before and during the lifetime of Jesus. What were they forbidden to do by their oppressors? You could illustrate this with a Roman soldier.

Under NEW EXODUS UNDER JESUS describe the death and resurrection of Jesus from the gospel of Mark. His suffering and death are the highpoint of the suffering of Israel. But he escapes from death. Show how he is like another Moses leading the people on a new journey. Illustrate this section with the two Christian symbols of the cross and the empty tomb.

Under NEW LIFE describe the new, changed life of people who share the resurrection of Jesus. This should include a description of some Christians who carry on the work of Jesus, in some way, in the world today. Your illustration could show one such person acting as a Christian towards a neighbor in need.

At the bottom of this poster use the heading EUCHARIST and describe the sacred meal celebrated by Christians. Show how the Mass recalls and brings into the present the New Exodus of Jesus. Illustrate this section with a group of Christians celebrating a Eucharist.

Groups who have completed their two posters could now place them side by side and explain the similarities to the whole class.

• Compare the suffering of the Jews in Egypt with the sufferings of the Jews under the Greeks and Romans and the sufferings of Jesus.

• Compare the Exodus under Moses with the New Exodus under Jesus. Were the early Christians correct in saying that Jesus was a New Moses?

• Compare the New Life of the people of Israel in the land of Canaan, with their Temple, with the New Life of Christians since the resurrection of Jesus.

• Compare the Passover and the Eucharist. They both bring the past into the present. What is similar and what is different about the two ceremonies?

Postscript

This book has covered an outline of the life of Jesus, particularly as that life was seen in the gospel of Mark. We must remember that the gospel of Mark is not a history book, just as this book which you have been using is not a history book. We may never know exactly what happened in the life of Jesus, much as we would like to know. But, we do know how the first Christians reacted to Jesus, what a deep impression he made on them. That is what a gospel is all about. That is what this book is about.

The book has also stressed the fact that Jesus was a Jew and that Christianity came from Judaism. The two religions might have continued side by side but that was not to be. Still, they have a great deal in common and each should respect the other. In particular, Christians should realize that without a knowledge of Judaism and a sensitive feeling for Jewish people they will never come to a real understanding of their own religion.

At some time in your life you should take the study of Jesus further. This book has simply given you a foretaste. Start with the gospel of Mark and then read Matthew and Luke (with the Acts of the Apostles). Finally read the gospel of John. You must keep in mind that these are ancient books that were first written in Greek and later translated into English. You will need some help to understand them. Even an adult cannot expect to pick up a gospel and read it with full understanding the first time.

What sort of help is required? You will need a good commentary, a book that explains the text piece by piece. Or you may prefer to study in a group under a guide who has been trained in Biblical Studies. Just as you know that one day you will need to know more about Maths and Science, so too you will need to know more about Christianity and Jesus.

But you have made a good start.

Glossary

Abraham. Abraham was considered to be the father of the Jewish people. He had been called by God while living in Mesopotamia to go on a journey to another land. This was the land of Canaan. Abraham had a son Isaac, and Isaac, in turn, had a son Jacob. Twelve of Jacob's sons were considered to be the founding fathers of the twelve tribes of Israel.

Angel. This word means a 'messenger'; when God delivers messages to human beings, he sends an angel.

Annunciation. This was the solemn announcement (which is what the word means) to Mary that she was to be the mother of the Messiah.

Assyrians. One of the peoples in northern Mesopotamia who became powerful after the time of David and Solomon. They destroyed the northern kingdom of Israel and its capital city, Samaria.

Babylonians. These were another people from Mesopotamia, from the south. They attacked Jerusalem in 587BCE and left the Temple in ruins.

Bar Mitzvah. This means 'son of the commandment'. It refers to the Jewish ceremony when a boy of thirteen is allowed to read from the sacred scrolls in the synagogue. From this time on the Jewish boy is bound to uphold the rules of his religion.

Bat Mitzvah. The same ceremony for a girl as bar mitzvah. Not all Jewish groups have this ceremony for girls. It means 'daughter of the commandment'.

Calvary. The Latin name for a hill outside Jerusalem where criminals were executed. It means 'place of the skull'. Jesus was said to have been crucified there.

Canaan. An old name for the land which the People of Israel occupied. The Canaanites were a people who lived in what was to become Israel before the time of Abraham.

Chuppah. This is the canopy under which Jewish weddings take place. Sometimes it is put up in the synagogue and sometimes outside it. It is said to signify the new home which the married couple are about to construct in their life together.

Circumcision. When a Jewish boy is eight days old the foreskin of his penis is removed with a knife. This is a Jewish religious ritual. The book of Genesis contains God's instruction for this to be done. The ceremony shows that the boy now belongs to the People of Israel.

Covenant. The word means a treaty or pact, in this case a treaty made between God and his people, Israel. Sometimes the word 'testament' is used instead of covenant. Christians maintain that God has made another treaty with them and they refer to this as the New Covenant or New Testament and the sacred writings of Christians are so called. Christians then use the term Old Testament to describe the Jewish writings which they share with the Jews. Christians should be aware that using the terms Old Testament and New Testament in the presence of Jewish people is offensive.

Crusaders. In the Middle Ages Christian armies, known as Crusaders or 'Cross bearers', came into the East to try to win back the Holy Land from the Arab people, who were mainly Muslim.

Eucharist. One of the names given to the sacred meal of bread and wine shared by Christians. It means 'thanksgiving'. Other names are the Mass, Holy Communion and the Lord's Supper.

Galilee. The area around the Sea of Galilee in the north of Israel where Jesus began his ministry. In the time of Jesus it was ruled by one of Herod the Great's sons, Herod Antipas, who was looked upon as being an evil man and a friend of the Romans.

Genesis. The first book of the Hebrew Scriptures. It tells the Jewish account of the beginnings of all things and the story of Abraham, Isaac and Jacob.

Herod. There were two Herods in the story of Jesus. One was Herod the Great, who had gained favor under the Romans and was given the title of King of the Jews. He was king when Jesus was born. Upon his death his kingdom was divided among three of his sons and one of them, Herod Antipas, was ruler of Galilee while Jesus grew up and began his ministry.

Holy Scriptures. This is the name of the great church in Jerusalem which is said to contain the tomb of Jesus as well as the hill of Calvary. It was built over the place where Queen Helena, the mother of Constantine the Great, was shown the tomb in the fourth century CE.

Jerusalem. The holy city of the Jewish people. Jerusalem had been captured by David from the Canaanites and made into the capital of a united people. David brought the Ark of the Covenant to Jerusalem and from that time it was a holy place. David's son, Solomon, built the first Temple in Jerusalem.

John. John was a gospel writer. His gospel was the last of the four to be written down.

Judea. The name for the area surrounding Jerusalem in the time of the Romans.

Kippa. The Jewish name for the small skullcap worn by Jews. Some Jews wear it all the time, others only when attending synagogue, sacred places or sacred ceremonies. It is a sign of devotion in the presence of God.

Luke. One of the gospel writers. His gospel contains one of the two accounts of the birth of Jesus.

Mark. Mark was a gospel writer, probably the first to write one of the gospels that we now possess. He begins his account with Jesus' ministry in Galilee.

Matthew. Matthew was a gospel writer. He, together with Luke, added an account of the birth and early days of Jesus.

Mesopotamia. This was the name given in Greek times to the land between the rivers Tigris and Euphrates. The word means 'land between the rivers'. This was the area from which Abraham travelled into Canaan and the land from which the Assyrians and Babylonians launched their attacks on Israel.

Messiah. The word means 'anointed one' and describes the great leader awaited by many of the Jews around the time of Jesus. The Messiah was expected to deliver the Jews from the forces of evil. Many present day Jews still await the Messiah. Christians maintain that Jesus was the Messiah.

Mount Sinai. In the biblical story this is the mountain where Moses met the God of Israel. Here God gave instructions for the way of life that the People of God were to lead.

New Testament. The name given by Christians to their sacred writings—the gospels, the letters of Paul and letters of other early Christians, the book of Revelation. It is called 'new' to distinguish it from the testament or covenant and the sacred writings of the Jewish people. It is impolite to use the term when speaking with Jews.

Passover (Pesach). The sacred ceremony of the Jewish people celebrated once a year and commemorating the escape of Moses and the People of Israel from Egypt where they were on the verge of destruction. The ceremony is still celebrated by the Jews and consists principally of a meal of bread and wine.

Persians. A people from the Persian Gulf region who overthrew the Babylonians under the great King Cyrus. They allowed the captive Jews to return to Jerusalem and to rebuild the Temple destroyed by the Babylonians. This was the Second Temple. This is the one that Jesus knew.

Pharaoh. A special title given to the kings of Egypt.

Rabbi. This is the title given to Jewish leaders and teachers both in ancient times and today.

Satan. This means the 'enemy'. When the Jews wanted to describe evil they described it in terms of a devil leader called Satan and a horde of followers, the demons. These spirits, they maintained, inhabited the world and sometimes even entered into people.

Seder. The word means a 'service' and refers most usually to the service performed at Passover by Jewish people.

Shabbat (Sabbath). The seventh day of the week, Saturday. According to the Jews God commanded this day to be kept holy, free of work, and dedicated to rest and prayer.

Shalom. This word is Hebrew and means 'peace'. It is the great hope of Judaism and Christianity that peace will come to all peoples.

Shema. A special prayer taken from the Hebrew Scriptures which acknowledges the oneness of God. It is said by pious Jews every day.

Sheol. A Hebrew word which describes a great cave under the earth where those who have died go. In ancient times most Jews would have known about Sheol. In modern times there are different beliefs among Jews as to what happens beyond death.

Synagogue. When the Jews became more widespread, in the period before Christian times, they found it difficult to have access to the Temple. Prayer houses, or synagogues, sprang up and they became the meeting place for Jews who wanted to study the Scriptures or to pray. Synagogues are the meeting places of Jews today, since the Temple of Jerusalem was destroyed in 70CE.

Tallit. A prayer shawl with tassels on the corners. It is worn by Jews when they pray. Some Jews wear a *tallit* under their shirt to indicate that they are always ready to pray.

Tefillin. Two black leather boxes attached to leather straps. Inside the boxes are pieces of parchment with special readings from the Hebrew scriptures. One of these boxes is tied around the head and the other tied around the left hand and arm when the Jew prays in a formal way.

Temple. The sacred place established in the city of Jerusalem where the God of Israel was said to have been present in a special way. The first Temple was built by Solomon and destroyed by the Babylonians in 587BCE. The second Temple was built with permission of the Persians and dedicated in 515BCE. It was beautified by Herod the Great and destroyed by the Romans in 70CE. There has not been a Third Temple.

Torah. This word describes the way of life laid down for the Jewish people by God. It includes the instructions on how to live a good life. It is sometimes translated as 'Law' but it is not simply a list of laws.

Index

(Page numbers in italics refer to topics appearing in small type on the page—activities or photo captions)

The Author

Robert Crotty is Associate Professor of Religion Studies at the University of South Australia. His studies have taken him to many places around the world—Theology in Rome, Biblical Studies and Archaeology in Jerusalem, History in Melbourne, the early beginnings of Christianity in Oxford. Among his educational publications are *Come Travel* (1969), *Prophets* (1980), *Symbols, Signs and Sacraments* (1982), *Introduction to the Gospels* (1987), *Finding a Way* (1991).

Robert has an abiding respect for Judaism. This present book reflects his concern that Christianity, together with its founder Jesus, be understood against their Jewish background and origins.

The Photographer

Michael Coyne is a photojournalist of international reputation. He is represented by the international agency, Black Star. He has worked on assignments for *National Geographic, Newsweek, Time, Life,* London *Observer* magazine and French and German publications.

He has most recently finished *A World of Australians*, featuring 70 portraits that illustrate the richness and variety of Australia's multi-ethnic society.

Acknowledgements

Many people have been involved throughout the long process of creating this book. In particular I would like to thank:

Fr Frank Moloney SDB, Catholic Theological College, Clayton
Rabbi John S. Levi, Temple Beth Israel, St Kilda
Dr Eugene J. Fisher, Secretariat for Ecumenical and Interreligious Affairs, Washington
Sr Shirley Sedawie and Sr Stella, Shalom Centre for Christian-Jewish Relations, Kew
Sr Myriane, Ecce Homo, Jerusalem
Sr Rose Theresa, Notre Dame de Sion, Jerusalem
June Marie Mason, Our Lady of Sion College, Box Hill
Fr John Keane, Holy Land Commissariate, Waverley
Fr John Chryssavgis, St Andrew's Theological College, Redfern
Catherine Hammond, E. J. Dwyer, Newtown
Mary Emery, Catholic Education Office, Adelaide
Graeme Barry, Catholic Education Centre, Brisbane
Sr Helen Giles, Catholic Education Office, Perth
Graham English, Catholic Education Office, Leichhardt
Pat Williams, Catholic Education Office, Parramatta